INDIANA
Curiosities

Help Us Keep This Guide Up to Date

Every effort has been made by the author and editors to make
this guide as accurate and useful as possible. However, many
things can change after a guide is published—establishments
close, phone numbers change, hiking trails are rerouted, facilities come under new management, etc.

We would love to hear from you concerning your experiences
with this guide and how you feel it could be improved and kept
up to date. While we may not be able to respond to all comments and suggestions, we'll take them to heart and we'll also
make certain to share them with the author. Please send your
comments and suggestions to the following address:

The Globe Pequot Press
Reader Response/Editorial Department
P.O. Box 480
Guilford, CT 06437

Or you may e-mail us at:

editorial@globe-pequot.com

Thanks for your input, and happy travels!

Curiosities Series

INDIANA
Curiosities

QUIRKY CHARACTERS, ROADSIDE ODDITIES &
OTHER OFFBEAT STUFF

Dick Wolfsie

The
Globe
Pequot
Press

GUILFORD, CONNECTICUT

Cover photos: (front and back) Dick Wolfsie; Dick with Barney (front)
by permission of The Photo People
Cover design: Nancy Freeborn
Text design: Bill Brown
Layout: Deborah Nicolais
Maps: XNR Productions Inc. © The Globe Pequot Press
Photo credits: All photos by the author unless otherwise noted.

Library of Congress Cataloging-in-Publication Data
Wolfsie, Dick
   Indiana curiosities : quirky characters, roadside oddities & other
offbeat stuff / Dick Wolfsie.— 1st ed.
    p. cm. — (Curiosities series)
   Includes index.
   ISBN 0-7627-2351-3
   1. Indiana—Miscellanea. 2. Indiana—Guidebooks. 3. Curiosities and
wonders—Indiana. I. Title. II. Series.
   F526.6W65 2003   2003043427

Manufactured in the United States of America
First Edition/Fifth Printing

*The prices and rates listed in this guidebook were
confirmed at press time. We recommend, however, that
you call establishments to obtain current information
before traveling.*

Contents

ACKNOWLEDGMENTS

This book was the hard work of many people, but mostly me. I'm the one who drove 6,000 miles, took 500 photos, and spent 100 hours on the phone and 400 hours on the word processor.

But knowing where to go, who to call and what to write about, well that's another story. Actually, it was over 200 stories.

Several ideas originated with the folks at WFYI, the PBS station in Indy. Their nightly show, *Across Indiana,* is a delight to watch and the producers were generous in giving me several leads. Bob Donaldson, anchor at Fox 59, does a segment called "Hidden Indiana." I thank Bob for his input.

Layne Cameron wrote several of the stories in the book and also acted as my analyst. Whenever I was panicked or depressed about some aspect of the book, Layne would call and tell me to relax. It was actually very annoying, but he was right. Thanks, Layne.

Then there are the countless people who heard I was working on the book and made suggestions of things they had seen in their travels. Those were probably the best of ideas of all.

And there's my wife, Mary Ellen. She encouraged me to take this project and built my confidence that I could do it. However, once I began writing the book, she didn't do anything to help. But she did miss me when I traveled.

To everyone who spent time showing me around their homes, their museums, their businesses, and their basements, my sincere thanks.

In writing this book, I visited most of the state's ninety-two counties. I met hundreds of wonderful people. It was a lot of fun.

But I'm glad it's over. It's nice to be back home again—in Indianapolis.

INTRODUCTION

You could write a book about what's not in this book. In fact, many people have written books about what's not in this book.

No, you won't find the Indianapolis Motor Speedway in this book or James Dean's home in Fairmont. Or French Lick. That's for those other books. And brochures. And tour guides.

Instead you will read about a man who painted a baseball 16,000 times and a guy who collects mousetraps. There's the minister who preaches at a drive-in theater. How about the woman with a front-yard rosary made of bowling balls?

No tourism brochure will tell you about the strangest house in Indiana. Or the man who holds the world record for blowing up hot water bottles.

Oh, there are a few exceptions. I threw in a few old favorites just to stay on speaking terms with the great folks at the Indiana Tourism Board who wouldn't mind if you went a few places and actually spent some money.

But for the most part, the stuff in this book will not be advertised on billboards to draw you off the highway exits. This is a book for people who like the quirky, the offbeat, and the unusual. If you have absolutely no interest in how to Astro-Turf your car or where to find the John Wayne Museum or a good frog race, you might want to buy one of those other books.

If this is a bookstore and you're just browsing, be careful. Here comes the clerk. This is NOT a library. Buy the book, stick it in your glove compartment, and begin driving. Have fun.

WHAT IS A HOOSIER?

*T*hose of you wondering about the origin of the word Hoosier are probably not Hoosiers. Debate on where this word comes from has raged for hundreds of years, with no definitive answer in sight. Was it a frontier term? Derived from a Briticism? Is it short for "whose ear?" or "who's there?" Who knows.

We accept the fact we are Hoosiers, just as people from Maine know they are Maniacs. Some things you just can't argue with.

Despite a request by my editor to unravel the mystery, I did not spend endless hours at the state historical society researching this thorny question. But for those of you with a thirst for knowledge, here's a bit of added lore.

Careful study suggests that more than 200 years ago when the land now known as Indiana was settled by folks of European descent, these early pioneers ran into groups of Native Americans they called "Indians." It is believed that this original confrontation may have had something to do with the word Indiana.

You can take that to the bank.

GREATER INDIANAPOLIS (AKA INDY)

Central Indiana is just crammed full of stuff that attracts millions of tourists to Indiana every year. But, as noted in the introduction, you won't find them in this book.

There's no RCA Dome or Conseco Fieldhouse in here. No Conner Prairie or NCAA Hall of Champions in here. You should visit all of these, of course, but when you want to see something well off the beaten path, grab this book out of your glove compartment and go for it. Or don't go for it, just read about it. Armchair travels can be fun.

There's the world longest slot car track and a store where you can buy 500 whoopee cushions. How about a man with a million corks in his basement? Or you can visit the world's only library in a mall or eat a four-pound hamburger. Meet the world's greatest apple picker. See a traveling circus sideshow or drive by the strangest house in Indiana.

Then relax and go to one of the few movie houses in America where you can watch a first-run movie and down a beer at the same time.

Yeah, Indy is full of famous stuff. This is the not-so-famous stuff. Unless this book changes all that.

PICKY FARMER
Indianapolis

If an apple a day keeps the doctor away, George Adrian won't need an HMO.

In 1980, on an apple-crisp day in late September, Adrian picked 30,000 apples (that's eight tons, 365 bushels) at his orchard. And he became, according to the *Guinness Book of World Records,* the fastest apple picker in the world. By the way, that's 1,000 pounds an hour.

Adrian is a third-generation apple grower, and when he heard about the record in the late 1970s, he saw no reason why he couldn't break it. Working with only a ladder and a picking bucket, Adrian used both arms as he twisted and contorted his body for eight straight hours, stopping only for lunch. Not to be picky (which he was), but he beat the old record by twenty-four bushels.

No one in the world is pickier than George Adrian, so says the Guinness Book of World Records.

Now, twenty-two years later, his record remains unbroken, though more than a few have tried to outshine the fifty-three-year-old Hoosier. Adrian claims that he has better technique now, but he has no interest in competing. "It's tough on the knees and the arms," admits Adrian, who says that after holding the record for more than twenty years, he'd be happy to give it up to a new crop of record-holders.

You can find George Adrian at his orchard most days at 500 West Epler on the south side of Indy. For the best apple cider ever (made fresh at the orchard), drop by or call (317) 784–0550.

TOTALLY WIRED
Indianapolis

W hen Bill Arnold was a young man, he dabbled in many different art forms. During one of his inspirational walks in the woods, he sighted a buffalo asleep (or dead) in the grass.

But it wasn't a buffalo. It was a heap of barbed wire discarded by a local farmer. Convinced this was an untapped source for artistic expression, Arnold crafted a life-size deer, the first of hundreds of creations that have made him one of the few "wire artists" in the country.

Arnold became so proficient that when he displayed one of his bald eagles on top of an Indiana billboard, motorists stopped to gaze at the national symbol, assuming it was real. People clapped their hands, threw rocks, anything to motivate the bird to take wing. Dozens even called the Department of Natural Resources to report the bird's apparent lethargy. "I think a lot of people have a photo of a wire eagle and think it's real," says Arnold.

Bill Arnold is one totally wired guy.

    Soon he crafted life-size creations for the Indianapolis Zoo as well as a bison to represent one of Indiana's largest banks. Today many of his creations stand outside corporate buildings around Indiana.

    Now working out of a downtown Indianapolis location, Arnold keeps the infamous wire eagle in a cage outside his studio. People leave him notes saying how cruel he is to keep a bird so regal locked in a cage.

Arnold's shop is open pretty much when he wants it to be, at 719 East St. Clair, Indianapolis. Check out his Web site at www.wiresoul.com.

M O N K E Y   B U S I N E S S
Indianapolis

Walk over glass, stick a nail in your nose, eat fire, swallow a sword!

Heck, that's just a day's work for Bart Simpson and the men of the Blue Monkey Sideshow.

These self-admitted masochists banded together about four years ago after doing a Halloween party and realizing the audience was tickled by anything that looked like it didn't tickle. "We realized that we were really doing a circus sideshow and the audience loved it. So we decided to develop some of those acts."

Simpson and his co-hurts researched the sideshow traditions, threw in a few of their own creations, and billed themselves as the Blue Monkey Sideshow. "The name lent itself to some great graphics," says Simpson, who can't wait to get up and go to work, assuming he can get up.

The Blue Monkey Sideshow has entertained (and grossed out) audiences all over the United States, but the group's home is in Central Indiana, where they work out of a garage in the historic Fletcher Place of downtown Indianapolis. They claim to be the only such sideshow in the Midwest and one of the few in the country, and you can see them at fairs, corporate functions, and colleges.

Don't try this at home. Or the office. A typical workday for the Blue Monkeys.
PHOTO: Katie Murphy/KMPD

Two of the Blue Monkeys have master's degrees, two are Shakespearean actors, and all of them love to live on the edge . . . and walk and sit on the edge, as well. "The Three Person Shrink-Wrap" is three guys sitting in a huge envelope of shrink-wrap while an assistant sucks the air out of the plastic material with a vacuum cleaner. The result is not pleasant to look at. Hey, it's a sideshow.

Bart Simpson also wants people to know that he is not related to the television character. Whatever that means.

Get more info at www.bluemonkeysideshow.com. We suggest you eat AFTER you look at their Web page.

WOOD BE ARTIST
Indianapolis

If you want to speak to Chie Kramer, YOU HAVE TO YELL. Why's that? Because most of the time this guy is in his shed brandishing a chainsaw. AND WHAT'S HE DOING? Hold onto your headdress. He's making Cigar Store Indians.

While Kramer was stationed in the San Juan Islands, he watched the native Indians craft beautiful totem poles. Years later when he was in college, a business professor asked the students to investigate an enterprise that was not in the Yellow Pages. Kramer, who up to that point wouldn't have touched wood carving with a 10-foot-pole, realized there was no listing for wood statue makers.

Kramer made a quick statue for the class, then another for a neighbor, who paid him cold hard cash for the little wooden Indian. Kramer was hooked. He hasn't looked back since. But looking down is a good idea, especially when you use power tools sixteen hours a day.

Beginning with a chainsaw, Kramer carves out the basic outline in about an hour, then fine-tunes his Indian with hand tools and a power grinder. Indians are painted by hand, always with authentic tribal colors. Total time for carving, painting, and drying can be a couple of months. Prices begin at $250.

Now, 2,500 Cigar Store Indians later, Kramer is one of the few wood carvers in the Midwest with this specialty. His work has been sold around the country, often to people with an interest in Indian history or some connection with cigars or tobacco. "The Cigar Store Indian," says Kramer, "is a true American icon."

Kramer doesn't want people just showing up at his house, so check out his Web site at www.cigarstoreindianstatue.com. But if you are on the northeast side of Indy, you'll hear him.

TOO PUNNY FOR WORDS

*I*ndiana-based insurance company American United Life has the two most popular signboards in Indianapolis. No joke. Well, actually it is a joke.

The company's two signboards have been providing Circle City residents with a wealth of witticisms for nearly five decades. They were the brainchild of then-Chairman Clarence Jackson and have been inspiring people to chuckle, guffaw, cheer, and, on occasion, even snort coffee through their noses since 1958.

Over the years, AUL has steered clear of inspirational sayings, political endorsements, and, generally, anything that's "too preachy." It has, however, made an art of humorous briefs without crossing the line into insulting or off-color. "We don't want people staring at our board so long that they have a car wreck," says Deborah Kingsmith, corporate communications coordinator (aka the Board Guru). "We go for ones that produce a groan or laugh on the spot."

Some of the highlights include:

Puns—Why isn't phonetic spelled the way it sounds? Do horse breeders strive for a stable population? Cross a vampire with a snowman and you get frostbite.

Definitions—Laughing stock: cattle with a sense of humor. Pacifier: scream saver.

Holiday Humor—Can't stop eating pumpkin pie? Try a pumpkin patch. Polite ghosts spook only when spooken to. Holiday blahs? Try Santa's elf-help tips.

Many of the featured phrases are submitted by outside sources. So if you have a pun or humorous definition, why not send it in?

Too funny for nerds. Hokey billboard humor from American
United Life, an Indiana-based insurance company.

You not only get the joy of seeing your thoughts in public, but you'll receive a whopping $5.00 check, thus proving the maxim: *Change is good. But dollars are better.*

Check out the signs at Vermont and Capitol and New York and Illinois. AUL's Web site: *www.aul.com/corporate/signboard.html.*

PUT A CORK IN IT
Indianapolis

Dom Garcia of Indianapolis has two million corks in his basement. But who's counting? Actually, Dom is.

A successful artist for many years, his passion for corks was stirred (not shaken) when he opened a bottle of expensive champagne and saw his name, Dom, as in Dom Perignon, emblazoned on the cork.

Soon Garcia was on a mission, cajoling people he met around the country (and the world) to send him corks. Now it is not uncommon for him to find boxes on his doorstep filled with corks, sent by waiters whom he was smart enough not to stiff.

Garcia divides the corks, separating the expensive ones from the synthetic variety. "Fine wines come with fine corks," he says, but even the cheap corks have a value to Garcia, who uses them to create works of art. And there's no stopping him, so to speak.

Over the years, Garcia has created a huge cork curtain (with hundreds of thousands of corks), clothing, the head of a bull, a giant spark plug, even a kitchen sink, all sculpted out of wine bottle corks. His most famous piece? The world's largest corkscrew, made of cork, of course.

Much of Garcia's artwork can be viewed at Gaia Winery in downtown Indianapolis at 608 Massachusetts Avenue, but an appointment is recommended by calling (317) 634–9463.

Putting a cork in it. Dom Garcia and his unstoppable hobby.

IDDNAT INTRESTING

*J*ohn Terhune is an Indianapolis chiropractor, and you'd
better bone up on your pronunciation before you pay
him a visit. Terhune has been listening to Hoosiers talk for
ten years and is convinced that the people of Indiana speak
a lean, economical language all their own, a language so
simple and easy to use that it is destined for worldwide
acceptance as "The New Global Language."

In his book, Why Hoosiers Can't Pronounce "Indianapolis,"
Terhune treats readers to 263 pages of words and their pro-
nunciations and definitions, Hoosier-style. In the book, you
will learn, for example, "Auzhusinkinat" is really "I was just
thinking that." Yes, there are hundreds of examples like this,
and just for the record, here is Terhune's list of eighteen different ways to say our capital city's name:

ANNAPLUS

ANYANAPPLES

ANYNAPLUS

ENGINEAPLUS

INDIANAPLUS

INDIAPLUS

INDIANAPOIS

INDIANAPPLES

INDIANAPLUS

INDYPLUS

INIANAPLUS

ININAPLUS

INNAPLUS

INNUNAPLUS

INNYNAPLUS

INYUNAPLUS

NNAPLUS

Terune also tells the reader which recognizable Indianapolis personalities are guilty of each of these linguistic
massacres. His explanation for the wide variety of pronunci-
ations? "Hoosiers have no use for a six-syllable word."

DON OF GUNS
Indianapolis

For more than a quarter of a century, Don Davis has been trying to convince people that he doesn't want to make any
money, he just loves to sell guns.

Well, that may be true, but that doesn't mean he hasn't made
any money. In fact, Davis, a former Teamster, admits to becom-
ing a millionaire in large part due to a silly slogan that began
because all his Teamster buddies wanted a discount at his gun
store. Davis told them that he didn't really want to make any
money, he just wanted to give discounts to his pals. He took a
sarcastic variation of that retort to the airwaves, and soon
became the best-known TV huckster in Indiana, maybe the Midwest.

When Davis first began in 1974 with a tiny gun and fishing
shop, he had a couple of grand in the bank. "At that time, my
goal was to clear fifty bucks a day and go fishing on Sunday,"
says Davis, who by the 1980s had two 10,000-foot gun ranges,
a residence in Florida, a home and golf course in Greenwood,
and assorted real estate. "I went from 300 a week to 300 an
hour," notes the gun dealer, who has never made any apologies
for his success. "In my wildest dreams, I never thought this
could happen. Only in America."

Davis has not been without controversy. At first, TV stations
shunned him. And when they finally did relent, they'd only put
him on after midnight. He might be the first TV spokesperson
to shoot a machine gun during his ads. He even performed in a
rock band to stimulate gun sales. All that, plus more jewelry
than a disco monkey, has made him a lightning rod for debate
between NRA enthusiasts and gun control advocates.

Davis believes everyone has a right to own a gun but thinks
people should be properly trained—and the gun registered.

Don Davis is loaded.

He's debated this issue on TV, radio, and college campuses. But it's no matter. He will always be known for that one slogan that turned him into an Indiana icon and a gazillionaire; "I don't want to make any money, folks, I just love to sell guns."

Davis is sometimes at his gun store at 3807 Lafayette Road in Indy (317–297–4242), but most of the time he's in Florida. And we're not giving you that number.

STORIED BUILDING
Indianapolis

The Fountain Square Theatre Building just east of downtown Indy (1105 Prospect Avenue) is on the National Register of Historic Places. It should also be listed, however, on the National Register of Magical Places (if there were such a list).

Its old-fashioned elevator, complete with attendant, acts as a time warp of sorts. It seems that each stop the Fountain Square elevator makes isn't so much a floor as it is a story. On the building's first floor, visitors step back into the poodle-skirt-wearing, black-leather-jacket-clad world of the 1950s. Here waits the Fountain Square Diner, a renovated Woolworth's diner complete with period movie posters and advertisements ("Try the Diner's Homemade Soups: They're Swell!") lining the walls while a Rock-Ola jukebox cranks out golden oldies.

The food is standard 1950s fare: hamburgers, jumbo tenderloins, fries, hand-dipped shakes, sodas, and sundaes. What's good? "You can't go wrong with a Fountain Burger, fries, and a chocolate malt," says Matt Schwartz, manager.

After dinner, you can jump on the magical vertical transporter and go down to the basement. Here the Atomic Bowl, a spoof of the era's nuclear bomb shelters, has seven lanes dedicated to duckpin bowling. Jerry Lee Lewis and Elvis croon over the clamor of the pint-sized pins and balls, while the malteds and cherry Cokes flow freely.

If the 1950s isn't your decade, ride up to the fourth floor and spend some time in the Roaring Twenties. Or you can return to the present and enjoy the modern-day view at the Rooftop Garden. Weather permitting, this is a great spot for cocktails or to watch the fireworks downtown.

DINNER AND A MOVIE
Indianapolis

It seems like a no-brainer. Build a movie theater where people can sit down and have a real meal and enjoy a glass of wine or a beer while watching the flick. You know, like dinner and a movie. Well, duh.

Ted Bulthaup had that dream, but the government said no. Up until the 1980s, city laws prohibited alcohol in a movie theater. (It wasn't moral, they said, but you could sit there with a Coke and watch violence and porn.) When the ban was lifted, the movie industry still frowned on the combination of movies and malt liquor, so Bulthaup had to sell his idea to skeptical studio bosses.

Bulthaup, who hails from Chicago, saw Indy as a good market for movie-goers, and the downtown area in the late 1980s was reviving and showing signs of great potential. Within a month of the Hollywood Bar and Filmworks opening in October of 1991, Bulthaup knew he had a hit. "After six weeks I was screaming directions to the long lines of people on the waiting list." Initially, Hollywood Bar and Filmworks featured second-run movies, but now moviegoers can see a first-run picture for $4.00, half the price of a major movie theater.

Enter the lobby and walk onto a Yellow Brick Road. Buy a ticket at a turn-of-the-century oak bank teller's cage, then approach the bar area through the Hall of Cartoons (lined with movie cels from Disney and Warner Brothers). The bar itself is a pretty darn good replica of the one in the movie *Casablanca*, and the walls are covered with movie stills from the classic age of Hollywood. Then there's the choice between one of three theaters, all with different films, each with state-of-the-art sound and film technology.

It gets better. There's a huge beer and cocktail menu and, for food, you can try such selections as the Meg Ryan Chicken Salad Sandwich (so named, says the menu, because she's a fox, and foxes love chickens), the Arnold Schwarzenburger, Oscar Fries, or the Potato Munch Skins.

Hollywood Bar and Filmworks is just Jay North of Union Station, Mae West of the Conseco Fieldhouse, Clint Eastwood of the RCA Dome. Call (317) 231–9250.

Big . . . As a House
Indianapolis

In the early 1960s, Jerry Hostetler's house was a couple thousand square feet, a modest ranch near downtown Indy. Now it's one of the biggest house in Indianapolis—55,000 square feet.

Even Hostetler isn't sure quite how it happened, but the house continues to grow, so much so that on any given day you can find as many as twenty-five workmen busy at their craft, tweaking Central Indiana's most-talked-about private home. According to one workman, Hostetler has a penchant for changing his mind from one day to the next about what he wants done to the house. It's not uncommon to move a wall or a bathroom. "It's okay with me," says one contented employee. "I work for Jerry 9 to 5 and I'll do whatever he wants."

The house has about fifty rooms, but Hostetler's not really sure exactly how many because "it's hard to tell when one room ends and another begins." Every room is furnished with priceless furnishings and artwork—all the result of Hostetler's extensive travel and his weakness for buying anything that strikes his fancy. "It doesn't have to be expensive," he claims, "just unique." Nevertheless, most of his china, crystal, statues,

*Jerry Hostetler's house! More rubberneckers every day
than a six-car pileup.*

and paintings have been shipped from overseas with little concern for expense. Floors and walls of imported ceramic and
marble complement every room. And the chandeliers . . . the
chandeliers are so magnificent you won't be able to take your
eyes off of them. But I'd recommend that you do. The center
staircase has no railing.

Most folks won't be able to see the inside of Hostetler's home,
which is pretty much reserved for friends and clients of his fire
restoration and construction business. "I want to showcase in
my home what I can do for your home," says Hostetler, who
admits to "a love affair with my house."

But folks can see the outside. In fact, it's not uncommon
for cars to back up for several hundred yards just gaping at
the Roman Gothic fountain with the five huge porcelain dol-

phins spouting water. At night, the fifty rooms are often lit, resulting in a surreal vision that has caused more than a few fender benders.

When Hostetler became tired of his half-dozen neighbors complaining about the traffic and the construction, he bought their homes. "Now I don't worry about the people next door complaining," he says, "because I own everything."

Hostetler claims the house will someday be done, but he admits that constant construction may always be necessary to make room for more acquisitions. He makes no apology for his obsession with beautiful things. "When in doubt," smiles Hostetler, "excess is best."

Want to see this place? Take Fall Creek Parkway to Kessler Boulevard in Indianapolis. You can't miss it. Even if you wanted to.

I N S A N E M U S E U M
I n d i a n a p o l i s

O kay, so you've just had lunch in downtown Indy and you have a choice. You can go see the best racecar track in the world, the best basketball stadium in the NBA, or the best minor league baseball park in the United States. All within a couple of miles.

But why? Especially when you can visit Indy's best-kept secret: the nation's only remaining nineteenth-century pathology building.

Now remember, this assumes you've had your lunch. Because inside the Medical History Museum you will see diseased brains, kidneys, and livers. There are antique X-ray machines, old stethoscopes, and assorted quack devices. In total, more than 15,000 medical artifacts. You can also stroll through the lab or the photography department or sneak a peek at the extensive medical library.

The facility was built in 1896 on the campus of Central State, a hospital for the insane, to use the nineteenth-century term. It was the second freestanding pathology unit built to serve a mental hospital. Today, it is the only remaining nineteenth-century pathology building in the United States.

Want a creepy feeling? Walk into the amphitheater where 100 years ago, medical students were lectured by professors who knew nothing of antibiotics or aspirin. They did know something about leeches. By the way, the first gallbladder operation was performed here by a Dr. John Bobbs in 1906.

The museum is at 3045 West Vermont Street, Indianapolis (317–635–7329) or you can reach it at Edenharter@aol.com. The co-pay to get in is $15. I mean, the admission.

PARTY TIME
Indianapolis

You're planning that big surprise birthday bash for your wife and you need 200 whoopee cushions, and you need them fast. Who ya gonna call? Kipp Brothers, of course.

The Kipp brothers of Germany are long gone, but their one-hundred-year-old dedication to novelty items has never wavered here in Indianapolis. Having been housed in a number of locations in downtown Indy, the company recently moved from its historic building that stretched five stories up (and one below). That was six stories chock-full of every imaginable novelty item: Slinkies, paddle balls, canes, hats, party favors, sunglasses, mugs, party favors, Hawaiian leis, cameras, cap guns, and toys.

Need a yo-yo? The new owner, Bob Glenn, can lay his hands on 4,000 dozen yo-yos without lifting a finger—except to his computer to see where they are in the warehouse. Huge quanti-

Kipp Brothers. A good place to buy one whoopee cushion.
A great place to buy a thousand.

ties of items, most of them imported from places like China and Korea, are purchased in thousands of grosses to start.

Needing more room, in fact, was what prompted Glenn to move from the old location downtown to a new location on the north side of town. His new building is 100,000 square feet, containing 38,000 different items, all listed in a 250-page catalog. If you can't find what you want, they don't make it. And if they don't make it, Bob Glenn can probably get it made. But here's a warning: It will be cheaper if you order a couple of million.

Of course, if you need just one whoopee cushion, a scenario hard to even imagine, Glenn does have a retail shop where patrons can see the novelties in shiny glass cases before committing to any particular item.

Glenn ships coast to coast, often filling huge orders, like a recent request for 30,000 purple bears. "After 9/11, I bought over a million flags. I won't be stuck with them," he says. "Patriotism will be hot for a long time."

Glenn never asks what people will do with some of their huge orders. "If it's legal, that's all I need to know," he says. "I mean, if you are going to rob a liquor store, you don't need 10,000 pairs of Groucho glasses."

Visit Kipp Brothers just west of Michigan Road on Ninety-sixth Street or contact them at sales@kippbro.com or (317) 814–1475. They'll send you a catalog.

LOONY RESTAURANT
Indianapolis

The Loon Lake Lodge is not a tribute to the movie starring Jane and Henry Fonda, but it is a tribute to the inventiveness of Chip Laughner, a local restaurateur, who dreamed of a theme restaurant to mimic the mountain fishing lodges of the Adirondack Mountains. "We wanted to provide a northern woods environment where people could relax and relive some childhood fantasies."

Laughner tore down one of his former cafeterias in the Castleton area of Indianapolis and rebuilt it with the outdoorsman in mind, creating several rooms like The Porch, The Trophy Room, The Lodge, and The Cabin, all decorated to reignite "the woodsman in all of us." Well, most of us.

You can spot the Lodge from blocks away by the hybrid Cessna airplane atop the roof, retrofitted with pontoons to add to the total fishing and hunting adventure. "We wanted to give the sense of people stopping at the lodge for a week or so,

Plane on the outside. Wild on the inside. The Loon Lake Lodge.

uninterrupted by the outside world," says John Ersoy, a partner in the business.

Once inside, your warm, cozy, safe feeling may be temporarily disturbed by the roar of a bear, the sound of birds, or the sight of a raccoon. Laughner installed state-of-the-art animatronics to delight kids and adults alike. "But we keep the effect subtle," says Ersoy. "We want you to enjoy the technology, but not have it disturb your meal."

The food is traditional, with a small part of the menu featuring exotic dishes like snake and elk. And if the wait is too long, there's always their retail store, an upscale shop where you can buy handcrafted hickory chairs or a chandelier made of elk antlers.

The Loon Lake Lodge is located at 6800 East Eighty-second Street. For details call (317) 845–9011.

LAWN DAY'S JOURNEY

*T*om Abeel was so impressed with the 1992 Clinton inauguration that he became a chairman. No, not a chairman of the Democratic Party. A chair man for the Woodruff Lawn Chair Brigade.

It was actually Abeel's wife, Linda, who had attended the presidential festivities. She then reported to her husband about a rather odd aspect of the parade: a group of men marching in unison with lawn chairs. Abeel immediately had a vision he couldn't shake. He saw his neighbors in a similar posture, marching the streets of historic Woodruff Place in downtown Indy. Abeel had no trouble recruiting "soldiers" for his brigade, but at the time he saw it as little more than a publicity stunt for some of their annual neighborhood events.

The brigade consisted of nine men dressed in casual attire with folded newspapers in their back pockets and lawn chairs in their arms. The brigade marched and one leader, a former major in the U.S. Army, barked signals. Every once in a while, the parade would cease, chairs would be unfolded, and newspapers drawn from back pockets. Their slogan: When the parade stops, we sit.

Before you knew it, Abeel and his crew were getting requests to march in other parades. The first big march was in, what else, March, the St. Patrick's Day parade, where Abeel was dumbstruck by the huge response his motley crew received when they rounded the corner to the applause of thousands.

The Lawn Chair Brigade. Unrest and rest, wherever they go.

After that, the group got so busy, they hardly had time to sit, I mean stand . . . whatever. They have performed in the Indianapolis 500 Festival parade, July 4th parades, and dozens of other events in and outside Indy.

The Woodruff Place Lawn Chair Brigade may be one of only a handful in the entire country, a dubious honor to say the least. But their motto says it all: Harmless Fun Since 1992.

R ETURNING TO THE MALL
Indianapolis

On any given weekend, there are a couple thousand kids hanging around the Glendale Mall in Indianapolis. But most are not at The Gap or Old Navy. Or playing video games.

They're at the library.

This library branch—part of the Indianapolis–Marion County system—is probably the only full-service library facility operating inside a mall in the United States.

The idea began a few years ago with three local issues: a neighborhood library was too small with no place to expand; a nearby mall was in search of a marketing concept to make itself more user-friendly for local families; the mall's huge, empty spaces were begging to be filled.

Enter developer John Kite with an idea so simple it was pure genius: "Let's put your new library inside our mall."

Maria Blake, director of communications for the library system, remembers a great deal of skepticism on the library board's part. "Library people are purists," reflects Blake, "so the idea of a library in a retail space took some getting used to."

Within just a few weeks of its opening, the Glendale branch of the Indianapolis–Marion County Library system was the busiest library branch in the entire county, handling a couple thousand people a day and almost twice that on the weekends. Research showed that people who had not gone to the old library were going to the new library, and in some cases they had never been to a library at all.

The library is open when the mall is open, allowing patrons to browse the shops for shorts or the shelves for short stories. The library has a full complement of computers, a Lego Mindstorm area for kids, a quiet reading room for adults, and a cafe for coffee and snacks. This is a long way from card catalogs and SHHH signs.

A final note if you're thinking of turning an old department store into a library. Books weigh much, much more than men's suits and ladies' dresses. So get a good structural engineer.

The library is easy to find. It's just south of Sixty-second on Keystone. Check it out.

ATLAS HUGGED HERE
Indianapolis

If you are looking for Tim Gravenstreter's store near downtown Indy and you can't find it, you may need a map. Actually, even if you can find it, you probably need a map. Because that's what Gravenstreter sells: maps.

In fact, that's all he sells, making his the only shop in Indiana selling just maps. Is this clear? Or do I have to draw you a map?

Gravenstreter, who used to build loft beds, had a lifelong love affair with maps. "Most boys my age looked at Mr. Atlas," says Gravenstreter. "I'd just look at an atlas."

When Gravenstreter opened the Odyssey Map Store almost twenty years ago, he had spent a sleepless week concerned that making a living selling only maps was "like opening a masking tape store." His fears were unfounded. "People came out of the woodwork," remembers the map purveyor.

Many of Gravenstreter's customers are vacationers planning a trip. Others are salespeople staking out territories, or outdoorsmen organizing a hike. Some are looking for antique maps for a collection. "There is no typical customer," says Gravenstreter.

Gravenstreter carries about 3,500 titles, so he can usually accommodate a request on demand. "Do you want a map of Iceland? No problem," brags Gravenstreter. But sometimes he must order from map publishers, especially for very specialized areas. Topographic maps for some remote regions, for example, are not on hand, but Gravenstreter can put his hands on about 600,000 different titles (maps) if he has to.

Gravenstreter also sells rare, antique maps and can show you Indiana maps going back to the 1830s. But he can't accommodate everyone. "We get a few requests a year for maps of the human body. That's not us," says Gravenstreter. "We go a lot of places, but we don't go there." There's probably more to tell you about maps, but I'm tired of typing Gravenstreter.

The store is easy to find, even without a map. It's on the corner of Ninth and Delaware, right near downtown Indy. Call (800) 972–1388 or you can E-mail tgravenstreter@hotmail.com. By the way, Gravenstreter helped with the maps for this book. That's why he sells the book in his store.

OPTICAL SOLUTION
Indianapolis

Verner Mabrey is a humble man. He never makes a spectacle of himself. But he does make them for other people. For almost a quarter of a century, Verner Mabrey has been the only person in Indiana to make a living just fixing eyeglasses.

His tiny store at 6021 North College Avenue in Indianapolis, the Optical Repair Shoppe, is a haven for people who have dropped, stepped on, or run over their eyeglasses. "Some people don't know which end to wear their glasses on," laughs Mabrey as he relates the number of people who have sat on their spectacles. "When asses meet glasses, I'm in business."

A sight for poor eyes. Indiana's only optical repair shop.

Mabrey has always been a tinkerer, repairing anything he could get his hands on. Looking for a new career in his late forties, he realized there was a niche for eyeglass repair. Most opticians didn't want to be bothered or the wait was endless. His tiny shop soon gained a reputation. And he got tons of referrals from the opticians because he did not sell glasses, only fixed them.

Mabrey fixes 4,000 pairs of glasses a year. The most common repair is a broken frame or temple. Many of his clients cannot afford two pairs of glasses so they wait an hour or so for same-day service. "Some of my customers can't find the chair to sit down," says Mabrey, whose patented logo is a pair of specs held together by a safety pin, a nail, and some tape.

Mabrey charges a flat $22 for most repairs. He has no computer, no fax machine, no receipts, no help, no nothing. Just a knack for fixing and a love of people. "I always ask people what they do," he says. "I learn something new every day."

The Optical Shoppe is at 6021 North College. Or talk to Mabrey at (317) 251–6629.

Rug-ged Cars
Indianapolis

Is it just me, or is it hard to find anyone nowadays to Astro-Turf your car?

Of course, there's always Henry Pelc of Indianapolis, who claims to be a rug salesman, but his real passion is covering cars and vans with indoor-outdoor carpeting.

Pelc claims that twenty-four years ago he had a dream—which probably isn't in the same category as Martin Luther King's dream—but it did motivate him to completely cover his 1969 GMC van with AstroTurf. Pelc won't describe the dream, but it was, well, auto-neurotic.

When others saw Pelc's finished product, his phone just rang off the hook. Okay, that's not exactly true, but he did have more than a few neighbors express interest in his concept. According to Pelc, folks like the idea because it protects the car if it's new and covers a multitude of sins if it's old.

Incredibly, the cars are covered in one piece of turf—no seams, just car doors and windows cut out. You pick your color as if you were in a carpet store.

Pelc has done cars, vans, parking bumpers, and the outsides of garages. He started charging $500 a car twenty years ago, but his prices have skyrocketed to $500 a car. "This is not for everybody," admits Pelc, whose latest design is a '97 van that was then airbrushed by a famous local artist.

And how do you clean an AstroTurfed car? "Well, you can go to a car wash," says Pelc, "or you can vacuum it. Either way, it's a conversation starter."

You can reach Pelc at (317) 898–4295.

DEAD AS A DOG
Indianapolis

Memory Gardens is certainly not the inspiration for Stephen King's *Pet Sematary*. This pet cemetery is much too pleasant and peaceful. And none of the animals buried here have ever arisen from their graves to haunt their owners.

The graveyard, located along the busy corridor of Indianapolis's Pendleton Pike, is certainly a respite from the sprawling restaurants, motels, gentlemen's clubs, and gas stations. The ten-acre spread was established more than fifty years ago by Leona Frankfort. After retiring from the Indianapolis Police Department as a dog pound superintendent, Frankfort bought the property and opened up an animal shelter. The cemetery later proved to be a logical extension of the kennel.

More than 5,000 animals are interred here. Not surprisingly, most of the deceased are dogs and cats. There are, however, parakeets, rabbits, and even monkeys. Tombstones with engravings that read "Dixie Frankfort" and "Heather Klotz" may lead visitors to believe they're strolling through just another graveyard—for people, not pets. That thought is dispelled quickly, though. It doesn't take much effort to spot markers with names such as "Sugar," "Scampy," "Wah Wah," and "Pouchie."

Pet owners don't seem to mind shelling out a few hundred dollars (depending on the animal's size) to preserve the memory of their four-legged and two-legged friends. One lady, who lives in California, has five plots here. Whenever one of her pets passes on, she lays it to rest at Memory Gardens.

Now that's a true animal lover.

Memory Gardens is at 9055 Pendleton Pike. Call at (317) 895-9055.

A REAL PHONE CARD
Indianapolis

So you have an old pair of gym shoes from 1984 and you just can't bear to throw them away. I mean, after all, you made three straight free throws in those high-tops. Don't toss 'em; make one into a phone.

Visit the Custom Phone Shop in Indianapolis and talk to Mike Irwin. He's the genius behind this unique concept. "I don't know of any place in the country where you can walk in off the street, hand a guy your old baseball mitt, and have it made into a phone."

When he first got into the business, he sold his products cheap, trying to compete with the mass-produced novelty phones, which were generally dull and uninspired. But when his creations started showing up in New York City art galleries, he knew he was onto something. "Our phones are functional art," says Irwin, who admits that many of his phones are often more conversation pieces than mouthpieces. And now assembly–line produced novelty phones are, more often than not, knockoffs of his earlier creations.

Irwin now does a big Internet business, catering to folks who want to create personal memorabilia or people in search of

Mike's slogan: "Hey, this phone's for you."

the perfect gift. Prices range from a couple hundred to $5,000. "That's if you want us to make a phone out of a diamond ring," says Irwin. "Of course, if you supply the ring, it gets a lot cheaper."

Irwin has made phones out of liquor bottles, softballs, golf balls, musical instruments, and stuffed animals. His favorite: a phone made from the racing helmet of an Indy driver. There is no limit or restriction on what he can and will do, which is why some of his work cannot be legally displayed in the window of his store in the mall. But most of his stuff is in good taste. So can Irwin make you a functional work of art out of your old gym shorts? Get on that old, dull, drab thing that you call a phone, and call him at (800) 783–6385 or visit his Web site: www.customphones.com.

BOARRR . . . ING

Who's the biggest bore at the state fair every year? Hard to tell. But the biggest boar? Well, that's easy. Bart Stuckwisch, co-owner of Hurricane, dubbed by the state fair as the world's largest boar, didn't raise Hurricane for the money. He did it for the fun. "Some guys like to race cars. Some like to do tractor pulls," quips Stuckwisch. "We like to raise large boars."

Hurricane, a 1,205-pound Yorkshire, won the title in 2001 and has a good chance to be the repeat champion for many years. Stuckwisch said the husky hog showed potential for bigness at an early age. "You have to have a really long boar," he says, "so you know he'll have the frame to handle the bulk."

The prestigious title comes with a purse of $450. That was mere chicken feed in terms of, well, chicken feed. The prize money doesn't even come close to paying for Hurricane's food bill. The burly boar eats mostly corn, and plenty of it. From his private 10-by-25-foot pen, Hurricane not only consumes the traditional slop but has also demonstrated a penchant for pies. "When you shake a Hostess wrapper," says Stuckwisch, "he comes running."

Run?

Apparently, Hurricane is amazingly agile—especially when enticed with cupcakes and fruit pies. Or maybe his agility can be credited to another of his favorite treats. "He takes a drink of beer now and then," says Stuckwisch. "He likes Busch Light."

We'd have thought he'd have preferred Hamm's.

Hurricane weighs more than 1,200 pounds with winds up to . . .
well, never mind.

PLEASANTLY PLUMP
Indianapolis

To someone passing through the Broad Ripple area of Indianapolis (6416 Cornell Avenue), it looks pretty much like any bar and restaurant. Even the name, Plump's Last Shot, seems like some veiled reference to a guy's last drink.

But this is no ordinary restaurant. It's a testament to what can arguably be called the greatest moment in Indiana sports. The "last shot" refers to Bobby Plump's final toss of his high school basketball career. A shot that has made Plump a living icon for almost fifty years.

In 1954 the little town of Milan, defeated the giant Muncie Central 32–30 at Indy's Hinkle Fieldhouse in what has become the quintessential David and Goliath story. Not that the Milan kids were losers. They had gone to the Final Four just the year before, but the idea of defeating big, bad Muncie seemed a bit remote.

To make a long story short (something that Plump has been unable to do for five decades, to the delight of hundreds of thousands), there were only forty-eight seconds left in a tied game. Plump took the ball and held it for what must have been an agonizing half minute, then called time-out. Coach Marvin Wood gave Plump his final marching orders, commanding the senior to "hold the ball 'til there were five seconds left, then dribble to the basket or take a jumper." Plump complied, faked left near the foul line, and shot himself into legendary status.

Plump says that 90 percent of the people in Indiana either watched that game on TV or heard it on the radio. Or said they did. When the team returned to Milan from Indianapolis, there were 30,000 people there to greet them—not bad for a city of one thousand. "I never tire of telling the story," says Plump. "What a rare opportunity it is for someone to talk about their formative years and have so many interested listeners."

Plump's last call at Plump's Last Shot.

Fifty years later, the original team still meets every year (one player and the coach are deceased), and Plump is still asked to recount those moments from a half century ago. In case you've been living in a cave (or Muncie, where the tale doesn't have the same glow), the movie *Hoosiers* is based on this bigger-than-life story.

Oh yeah, and that restaurant. In addition to good food, it's chock-full of basketball memorabilia and there's even a video showing that final shot, faded and blurred though it may be. Owner Bobby Plump is often there. But where would he be today if he had missed the jumper? The late curmudgeonly sportswriter for the *Indianapolis Star,* Bob Collins, said that Plump "would be pumping gas in Pierceville."

"I don't think so," says Plump with a smile, "but let's just say I'm glad I made the shot." Plump says he's seen quite a few bad calls in his day. Here's a good one: (317) 257–5867.

SIGN HERE
Indianapolis

If you want an autograph of baseball hurler Dwight Gooden, there are a gazillion places to go in Indiana. If you want Dwight Eisenhower's signature, you need A Rare Find Gallery and Steve Nowlin, who calls himself a historic document dealer. "I used to say I was a philographer," says Nowlin, "but people wanted to know why I wasn't in jail."

Nowlin, recognized around the country as one of the few people who can authenticate autographs, first got hooked fifteen years ago while looking at a signed letter from Louis Pasteur. "Something just clicked," says Nowlin, who quickly became intrigued with how autographs are verified.

Steve Nowlin knows what your autograph is worth. Probably nothing. Sorry.

Nowlin's first acquisition was a Robert E. Lee, which he bought for $540 and sold for $1,200. Years later the autograph was worth almost $5,000. Then he was really hooked. He has a huge historic reference library with signature facsimiles, as well as information about different types of paper and ink. Collectors often fax photocopies of signatures to Nowlin for a preliminary assessment.

Inside Nowlin's shop you can find the signatures of everyone from Benjamin Franklin to Laurel and Hardy and Elvis Presley. Virtually all autographs are displayed in decorative frames with accompanying photos and other memorabilia. His personal favorite is a Paul Revere, valued at over $50,000. At any given time, Nowlin has several autographs of every U.S. president.

Nowlin is not infallible (although he does have autographs of several popes who are). He once bought an autograph of Sitting Bull, later to find that the signature was a fraud. In the picture, Sitting Bull was standing. "That should have been a clue," says Nowlin.

To have your autograph authenticated on your credit card receipt, stop by 942 Fort Wayne Avenue in Indianapolis, or call (317) 822–4159.

ARMS TALK

As general aviation pilots fly over Fred Ropkey's farm in Central Indiana, they can't help but notice an unusual assortment of historic yard art. What they are seeing is one of the nation's largest private collections of American armored and tactical fighting vehicles.

Ropkey's eighty-acre farm on the outskirts of Indianapolis is home to scores of tanks, fighter planes, artillery boats, jeeps, combat boats, motorcycles, and cannons—all from World War I and II, Korea, Vietnam, and Desert Storm. There's even a shuttle module from a recent space flight. Everything, yes everything, must be in working order, although Ropkey purposely dismantles all weapons for safety reasons.

Ropkey, a Marine tank officer during the Korean War, started his collection with a War of 1812 sword when he was just seven years old. Now sixty-five years later, his collection is so vast that moviemakers keep his name in their Rolodexes. If you saw the movies Blues Brothers, Tank, The Siege, or Mars Attacks, you saw some of Ropkey's little babies. His tanks and planes have been seen on the Learning Channel and the History Channel.

Priding himself as a military historian, Ropkey can spin a true story about every piece of equipment he owns. Virtually everything is saved from oblivion when he and his associates rescue items about to be salvaged. "At one time, the government didn't care about this stuff," he says. "Now they want to acquire the very pieces I own for their own military museums."

One prized possession, a cannon from the battleship Arizona, had been removed from the ship just months before its journey to Pearl Harbor. Ropkey discovered the cannon at a junkyard about to be sold for scrap. "I save these items for posterity; they are part of history," he says. "Some of this stuff would have been lost forever."

Ropkey's collection is open to the public, but he doesn't like to advertise that fact, so if you wander onto his property between 10:00 A.M. and 4:00 P.M. on weekdays, you can look around. But Ropkey doesn't want his phone number or address in the book. He says if you really want to see his place, you'll find it.

Hey, I don't argue with a guy who owns twenty-five tanks.

Armor star Fred Ropkey in his backyard. Defense without da fence.

TALKING TRASH
Indianapolis

One home's trash is Tim Harmon's treasure.

Harmon, owner of Tim and Billy's Salvage Store, likes to stay one step ahead of demolition crews. Before a wrecking ball destroys an aging home, he works feverishly to salvage doors, windows, mantels, hinges, tubs, toilets (outhouses, too), and, yes, even kitchen sinks. "I'll work on a house until my fingers ache," says Harmon. "Sometimes I'll leave and later turn around and come back because I feel guilty about leaving something behind."

The joy of the find is second only to the joy of the sale. His customers include people restoring old homes, new-home builders looking to add vintage charm, and others simply wanting to give their abodes a touch of old-fashioned decor. "We have everything that no one else has," boasts Harmon.

His store in Indy is littered with endless aisles of salvaged materials—a pack rat's dream. There are more than 400 solid wood doors, 600 sets of claw feet (for bathtubs), piles of ornamental bricks, shelves of kitchen cabinet hardware, boxes of cast brass locksets, an assortment of fireplace mantels, scores of barn beams, and scads of lead-glass windows.

Some salvage is rather famous, such as the bathtubs from the West Baden Springs Resort. It was the common commode, however, that netted Harmon's shop national media exposure. Writing about the revolt against water-conserving toilets, *Time* magazine cited Tim and Billy's, at 2442 Central Avenue (317–925–6071), as a gray-market supplier of old-fashioned, "full-flush" toilets. The high-profile story boosted sales to customers from around the country, making Harmon flush with pride.

PLAYING THE SLOTS
Indianapolis

Three times a year, drivers flock to this world-class racetrack to vie for the title of champion. Indy, NASCAR, and Grand Prix cars all race here. And you can too, if you have $15 and your own slot car.

Huh?

Indy Slots is not the fabled Indianapolis Motor Speedway, but it is the longest 1:24 scale slot car track in the United States. "The only one longer than ours is in Brazil," says George Butler, manager.

The southside slot car center has three 1:24 scale tracks, with its crown jewel being the 235-foot Ogilvie Hillclimb. The expansive course has seven turns, two levels, and eight slots. And according to Butler, the track's dogleg turn is deadly. "The good drivers know how to get in and out of that corner and the others," he says. "It's as much watching as it is listening."

Attempting to watch a car complete a circuit is enough to cause vertigo. That's why veteran racers simply stare at a single turn during a competition. They'll *see* when to ease off the gas in some corners, and they'll *hear* when to slow down through others.

Instead of racing for a Borg-Warner trophy and a drink of milk, competitors race for plaques and a small payoff. It's certainly not enough to pay for their cars, their controllers, or all of their speed-enhancing modifications. To them, though, it's kind of like those MasterCard commercials:

Slot Car: $35 to $200

Controller: $50 to $300

Satisfying the need for speed (even on a 1:24 scale): Priceless.

Indy Slots is located in Indianapolis, south of I–465 at 5135 South Emerson. For more information call (317) 787-7568.

RELEASING INFORMATION

*I*n 1976, Bill Shirk, a thirty-year-old radio DJ from Indianapolis, went to Pamplona, Spain, strapped on a straitjacket, and ran in the streets. He was hit head-on by two bulls. It was all part of Shirk's master plan to become the best escape artist in the world. He soon became the best known, making it into newspapers throughout the world for his apparently reckless stunt. Then Shirk was off to Mexico, where he dove off a 150-foot cliff, again in a straitjacket.

His career had begun only a year or so earlier when he was supposed to chicken out of a stunt involving a straitjacket as a part of a radio promotion. But instead Shirk got hooked (or unhooked, I guess) on escaping and began a dedicated pursuit to learn more about the art of self-extrication.

Inspired by Harry Houdini, Shirk began developing more and more of his own escape tricks. Before long Shirk was hanging upside down or being buried alive in his straitjacket all over the country. In 1979, he hung from a helicopter in a straitjacket while ABC recorded his record-breaking escape. In 1981, he buried himself in the ground for seventy-nine hours with two tarantulas, a rattlesnake, and a 10-foot python. Hey, I'm not making this stuff up.

In 1991 Shirk spent fourteen days underground in a coffin. No food, just water, and a telephone so he could talk to reporters around the world. In 1993 Shirk was handcuffed, chained, and put in a Plexiglas coffin, then buried under seven tons of concrete. Can you imagine being married to this guy?

The stunts continue—he is already planning new escapes. Shirk's now president of a radio broadcasting company, but even at age fifty-six, he hasn't slowed down, always looking for another way to prove he's one of the best escape artists in the world.

By the way, his secretary thinks it's cute to say that he can't talk because he's tied up at the moment. It was funny the first time.

Bill Shirk: heels over head in love with danger.

PHOTO: Anthony Villainis

Tuckaway
Indianapolis

I t would be hard to find a house in Indiana more steeped in
mystery and more alive with history than a place called Tuckaway. If you want to know what life was like in the first half of
the century, this is the place.

From 1910 through the 1940s, this forestlike bungalow was
the home of Nellie Simmons Meier, a pint-sized patron of the
arts with a penchant for palm reading, who hosted a throng of
stars looking for a guided tour of their future. Nellie was not a
psychic. She never claimed to tell the future, but instead she
made observations about the person after analyzing the lines
on their palm, then combining that with research into the person's character and history. She was probably just as accomplished at reading people as she was at reading their palms.

Her client list was impressive: Walt Disney, James Whitcomb
Riley, George Gerhswin, Booker T. Washington, and Helen
Hayes, to just drop a few names. Legend has it that Nellie
pleaded with Carole Lombard not to board the plane that would
eventually crash, a clear departure from her claim that she did
not predict futures. Nellie even read the palm of Albert Ein-
stein. Oh yeah, and Eleanor Roosevelt.

Walk into the massive drawing room with a 15-foot ceiling
and gaze upon original autographed photos of past clients,
each with appropriate thank-yous. The present owner, Ken
Keene, an expert on the restoration of historic properties, has
re-created the generation's mood with Persian rugs, Victrolas, a
grand piano, fringed shades, and shaded lamps. Those who
have been there say the entire atmosphere lends itself to conversation about this world and the next.

*Nellie Simmons Meier's parlor, where everyone
gave her a hand.*

Tuckaway is not open to the public, but Keene does allow
nonprofit organizations to hold fundraisers there, in the spirit
of Nellie herself who donated her palm-reading assets to charity. In addition, Keene will occasionally rent out to private parties. But for the most part Tuckaway remains unknown,
though it's located just a block off the main drag of Thirtieth
and Meridian.

Nearby residents can get a look via the annual neighborhood
house tour, but for many reading this story (you may be one),
you're learning about Tuckaway for the first time.

KING OF SANDWICHES
Indianapolis

H erb Howard has the biggest buns in Indiana, maybe in the whole country. He needs them. His restaurant, Supersize Sandwich Shop, serves a four-pound hamburger—six pounds when you add all the trimmings. The cost of this beefy delight is very reasonable: It's free. Providing you can eat it all by yourself in two hours. And the fries and a large Coke. Burp!

Howard, a former construction worker, claims he's had hundreds try and only a handful succeed. One 490-pound gentleman completed the task in forty-five minutes and vowed to be back the next day. "I haven't seen him since," says Howard, who now offers an additional fifty dollars for successful completion of the herculean task. "Everyone thinks they can do it, but I don't shell out many fifty-dollar bills," he says.

The burger, which is 12 inches in diameter, sits atop a specially made bun that the baker calls a UFO. Howard grills the burger in four sections so that families can share it. Average cooking time is just under an hour.

For most families, the patty serves four to six people and costs $18. Patrons can also opt for more normal-sized treats, and Howard is proud of his supersized tenderloins and Philly steak sandwiches. Everything is big but the shop; it's a former liquor store located on the corner of Thirty-eighth and Kessler.

Howard's business has boomed as word has spread of his free-meal deal. Says Howard, when asked to compare his product to the competition down the street: "If you want a snack, get a Big Mac."

For takeout call (317) 916–0379. Eat hardy.

Indiana's biggest burger at the Supersize Sandwich Shop.
More fat than the federal budget.

MUSIC TRIP

*W*hile reading the local Indianapolis newspaper, limo driver Craig Curless saw a photo of a cab driver in Korea crooning to his passengers.

Curless knew that karaoke was popular at many nightspots in Indy, so he thought why not transfer the idea to his stretch limo? Curless got permission from his boss at Carey Indiana Limousines to retrofit his vehicle with speakers, microphones, a CD player, and a TV screen. Before you could say Madonna, Curless had created Indy's first and only singing limo. It may be the only one in the country.

That was ten years ago and since then Curless has combined a lot of good driving with a lot of bad singing. It's mostly junior high and high school kids who rent his limo, but more and more baby boomers want to belt out "Love Shack" on the beltway. As Curless motors down the street to Motown tunes, voices from inside the limo can be heard outside for blocks. Occasionally passengers prefer to use the mikes to share their personal thoughts with pedestrians, rather than sing. "We frown on that," says Curless, "but as long as what they say is in relative good taste, we tolerate it."

You can call Carey Indiana Limousines at (317) 241–6700.

WALLFLOWER
Indianapolis

Tori Allen is not a typical teenager. She's not making her mother and father climb the walls. She's doing it herself. And doing it awfully well. By just about every standard you can apply, Tori Allen, at just five feet tall, is the best indoor women's rock climber in the United States, with a roomful of trophies to prove it.

Tori climbed her first wall in 1999, amazing onlookers and her own parents, who were smart enough to see great potential in her scaling abilities. She entered her first competition a few weeks later and followed it up with a virtually unbroken string of victories for the next three years.

Tori's miraculous agility and strength were clear to all. So clear, in fact, that parents Steve and Shawn Allen purchased a local climbing gym that had fallen into disrepair. Along with her brother Clark, who is also a national champ, Tori has given the sport a much needed shot in the arm. And legs.

In September of 2001 Tori became the youngest woman to scale the nose of El Capitan in Yosemite National Park (her second outdoor world record in climbing). And to think her parents only wanted her to go outdoors and get some air.

Both kids are blessed with incredible poise in a demanding sport where the competition is intense, with everyone trying to scratch their way to the top. By the way, those who know say Tori is also headed toward being Olympic material in the women's pole vault.

Want to see Tori and Clark in action? Check out Climb Time Indy in Fishers, or its other location on the west side of Indianapolis (317–596–3330). The sister-brother combo is often there after school giving advice or doing demonstrations. Once you get there, the real reaching begins.

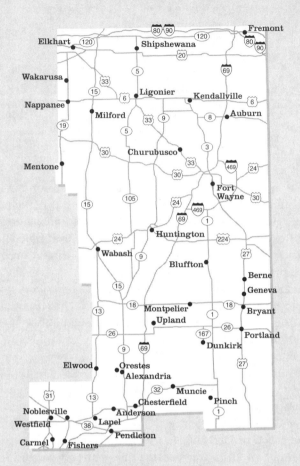

NORTHEAST

NORTHEAST

You can reach most of the places in this section within a couple of hours of Indianapolis. And it's worth every minute. What a great group of one-of-a-kind museums, oddball collections, and quirky people!

Don't miss the biggest collection of fruit jars in the world, a barn covered with 3,000 wrenches, the world's biggest apple pie, or the smallest children's art gallery. There are singing firemen and giant Indian statues. Half of one city is painted on a cement wall.

Is your head spinning? Visit one of the few windmill museums in the country or relax in Pinch, population three. Sorry, no hotels. Tense? Try Camp Chesterfield, where you can kick back and chat with a long-lost relative. Or try skating on artificial ice or stop by a farm in Alexandria and see what happens when you paint a baseball 16,000 times. I painted it once myself.

No, you won't be overwhelmed by the scenery, but there's lots to see that you won't find in most guidebooks. Some stuff is hard to find, so ask the locals. That's how I discovered most of this part of the book.

Brush with Greatness
Alexandria

Mike and Glenda Carmichael have been married thirty-two years and still have a ball. In fact, they've had the ball for twenty-five years. A paintball, that is.

It all started in 1977 when Mike and his three-year-old son, Michael Jr., painted a baseball. Mike, a painter by trade, thought it would be a fun pastime for his family to continually repaint the ball to see just how big it could get.

Nobody has painted a baseball more than
Mike Carmichael. Well, nobody that has admitted it.

Fast forward two and a half decades and more than 16,000 coats of paint. Now you have a 550-pound sphere of paint, the size of a huge beachball. Yikes! And there is no end (or circumference) in sight.

Mike has the paintball safely tethered to the top of a barn where it sways ever so gently as neighbors come by to apply a fresh coat. He keeps a log of all visitors and carefully tracks how many coats of paint have been applied, as well as the specific colors used. "We've had people from all over the country and even a few foreign visitors," says Mike, who's not sure how people find out about his oddity. No doubt being in *Ripley's Believe It or Not* is part of the explanation, and of course it's hard to keep something like this quiet.

Glenda, herself, is responsible for more than 8,000 paint coats, a feat for which she is openly proud. "It's more fun than vacuuming and you feel like you have accomplished something." You have?

Mike is a pretty friendly guy, but don't just drop in. You can call him if you're up in Madison County, near Alexandria (765–724–4088). You might or might not get the brush-off.

SCHOOLHOUSE ROCK
Anderson

Elvis has left the building—and he's driving a school bus!

Paul Butler has been impersonating Elvis Presley since he was four years old. After "being" Elvis for more than thirty-six years, the Anderson native admits that there is no venue in which he won't appear—and that includes school buses.

The forty-year-old has sung at weddings, reunions, bars, and fairs. Young Madison County residents, however, believe his best performances were delivered while driving them to school. "I dress up sometimes for my kids on the bus," says Butler, member of the Professional Elvis Impersonators Association. "We'll go down the road singing Elvis. It's really something to hear sixty kids singing, 'You Ain't Nothin' but a Hound Dog.'" The self-proclaimed "King of the Road" even impersonated Elvis while driving an ice-cream truck. ("You want a peanut butter and nanner ice-cream sandwich, kid?")

Making kids smile is one of Butler's greatest joys. Performing in Memphis, though, ranks right up there, too. He gives nearly 150 shows each year, but his favorite is the annual performance in Presley's hometown. "There are 35,000 Elvis impersonators in the world," says Butler. "The city of Memphis had never paid for an impersonator to do a concert. I was the first."

It would be tough for Butler to choose between leading a school bus choir or performing in Memphis for the likes of Priscilla and Lisa Marie. Luckily for him, he can do both. It's good to be the King.

To book the King for a show, call (765) 644–8185. Thank you. Thank you very much.

*A**uto** E**xotic***
Auburn

This museum is a duesy, no doubt about it. It's the Auburn Cord Duesenberg Museum in Auburn. Just drive your pathetic 1994 Ford Taurus to the intersection of State Road 8, 20 miles north of Fort Wayne and 35 miles south of the Indiana Toll Road, and you're 98 percent of the way there.

Heaven on wheels. Go to the museum, because you can't afford to buy one.

Once inside this 1930 art deco building (the former head-quarters for the Auburn Automobile Company), prepare to drool over the world's most glamorous automobiles—including the Auburn, the Cord, and the Duesenberg. But this museum does more than display pretty cars. Its mission is to take these icons of the classic car era and beyond and put them into historical perspective. Cars are displayed in galleries that help the patron understand the impact that luxury motoring had on the automobile industry and the nation as a whole.

The cars were more than fashion statements, however. They were supremely crafted engineering feats that allowed the driver to go 125 miles per hour while the lady in the back applied her makeup before the built-in vanity.

There are more than one hundred cars to look at, cars owned by the richest and most famous people in the world. See what Gary Cooper, Greta Garbo, and Clark Gable paid up to $20,000 to drive. Look at J. Paul Getty's 1932 Duesenberg J. Torpedo Convertible, the same type car driven by author John O'Hara. Over the years, the museum has featured cars owned by Elvis, John Lennon, Frank Lloyd Wright, and the Smothers Brothers.

A favorite is the Cars of Indiana Gallery, featuring autos of the past—manufactured in, of course, Indiana. Cars like the Revere, the Haynes, the Premier, and the Stutz, just to name a few of the more than 150 different brands produced in the Hoosier state.

Labor Day weekend is the Auburn Cord Duesenberg Festival, a collector and tourist favorite, and the largest event in Indiana outside of Indianapolis. Each year at this time, thousands of cars are auctioned off to hungry enthusiasts eager to buy a piece of history. In the past, autos belonging to Michael Jordan, Clark Gable, and even an armored car once used by Princess Diana have all been sold, commanding huge prices. Even the Batmobile from the 1995 movie *Batman Forever* changed hands to some caped collector for his cave. Also part of the festival is an antiques sale, quilt show, decorator showcase home, and downtown cruise-in. The year 2002 marked the fiftieth anniversary of the ACD, the Auburn Cord Duesenberg Club.

So bring your cameras to 1600 South Wayne Street in Auburn. The museum has virtually no restrictions on picture-taking. Lots of Dues, very few don'ts. For information call (260) 925-1444 or check its Web site: acdmuseum.org.

AMISH DELIGHT

*T*his book is full of neat photos, but don't expect to find one of Elizabeth Coblentz. Even though Mrs. Coblentz's column appears in ninety-five newspapers every week, she shuns the camera.

She's not shy. She's Amish. No photographs permitted.

Septuagenarian Elizabeth Coblentz, of Allen County, is known as the Amish Cook. She takes us not only inside her kitchen, but inside the Amish community, where readers can get a taste of her apple butter, as well as a sampling of a simpler, more tranquil life.

The column was not the idea of Elizabeth Coblentz. It originated with Kevin Williams, a nineteen-year-old entrepreneur from Ohio who—after writing a high school paper on the Amish way of life—conceived the idea of an Amish cooking column. But the business concept lacked a major ingredient in his recipe for success: an Amish cook.

Williams trekked through Indiana Amish country literally knocking on doors (there are no doorbells), until he found Mrs. Coblentz, who initially scoffed at the idea, but was gently convinced to take on the project.

Mrs. Coblentz is Old Amish—traveling by horse and buggy, cooking without electricity, and writing her column by candlelight. Her recipes are a mix and blend of good home cooking with stories about her husband and seven children. We learn about Amish life—a family wedding or a death in her family—in the very same column we are treated to a slice of Amish apple pie.

By the way, Kevin Williams is also marketing a line of Amish Cook Pies and has signed a deal with a major grocery store. Williams is not a Shaker, but he is a mover.

KRUSE CONTROL
Auburn

U sually when a person likes a museum, he becomes a member. Dean Kruse bought the place, instead.

Kruse's car collection at the Auburn Cord Duesenberg Museum and his nearby auto auction are already legend in Auburn. In 1999 Kruse became intrigued with an old military museum in Messancy, Belgium. The museum, which had been neglected and needed a new home, contained hundreds of priceless World War II vehicles. Kruse knew they had a place back in Auburn.

Maybe the best WWII museum in the world.
Tanks for the memories.

Once the museum was purchased, work began to ship the scores of military vehicles, forty rolls of battlefield film, and many cases of military uniforms and weapons from all major countries of the war. All of this is now displayed at the WWII Victory Museum, in a new 200,000-square-foot building just across from the Kruse Auction in Auburn.

Any standouts? You betcha: How about Adolph Hitler's personal parade car, replete with thousand-pound doors, triple bulletproof glass, and a reinforced floor? There's also General Eisenhower's parade car and General Patton's command jeep. All the military armor was researched and connected with real warfare. "We have material that was actually used in battle, not training vehicles like you see in many museums," says Kruse.

The museum is also kid-friendly, offering an opportunity for youngsters to win points through interactive games and then receive a rank when they leave the museum. All veterans are admitted free of charge. Head on up to Auburn on I–69, visit the Auburn Cord Duesenberg Museum first, then go down the road to the WWII Victory Museum. You can reach it at (260) 927-9144.

ACE IS NOT THE PLACE
Auburn

The really cool thing about Auburn City Hardware is that Abraham Lincoln could have bought an axe there. He didn't, but he could have. Why? Because Auburn City Hardware is 150 years old—the oldest continually operating hardware store (in the same location) in Indiana.

Founded in 1850 as Pioneer Hardware, the store has had about a half-dozen owners. The building was destroyed by fire in 1868 but was soon rebuilt. In 1932 E. L. Kokenge bought the nuts and bolts operation and in 1952 passed it on to his son.

Indiana's oldest hardware store. If they don't have it, they once did. But they've been out of it for 150 years.

Now, fifty years later, Robert Kokenge is still the crusty old proprietor of a store that can only be described as a step back into the past, and often a step back into a pile of sheet metal, leather straps, and antique rakes. "We do things the old way," brags Kokenge, who claims that if you want just one of something—like a battery—they'll break open the package. "'Course then we have to charge you for our time."

Inside the store is a range of products that spans pretty much the period between the Civil War and noon today. While modern appliances are readily available, you can also find a hundred-year-old meat grinder, pipe threaders, glass-cutting tables, belt-making machines, and canning jars. There are rocking horses, old trunks, and fifty-year-old cans of paint. "We don't do dynamite anymore," sniffs Kokenge. "The government thinks we shouldn't sell it and they know best." He was gritting his teeth when he said that.

There are no computers in the store, just a hundred-year-old National Cash Register and an adding machine. "I've been here fifty-three years," says Kokenge, "and nothing has changed." He was smiling when he said that.

There are other hardware stores in town, but eventually customers end up at Auburn City Hardware at 203 South Main Street (260–925–3610). A place where Ulysses S. Grant could have bought a hammer. He didn't. But he could have.

Pressing Information
Berne

When William Hauenstein emigrated to the United States from Switzerland in 1856, he had no plans to build the world's biggest cider press. But he did, in 1864, and it's still the world's largest. The press beam of this mammoth contraption is 30 feet long, hewn from a single, giant, white oak tree—a tree that was probably a sapling when Columbus arrived in the New World. Hauenstein used only hand tools, an axe, chisel, and hammer to fashion his creation.

The contraption weighs in at two tons and can turn thirty bushels of apples into one hundred gallons of cider with one cycle. Layers of straw are used to siphon out skin, seeds, and stems after the apples have been cut by the grinder wheel. Nowadays, the apple mush is siphoned through a type of cheesecloth, but the concept is similar.

The press worked on and off for more than one hundred years at its original forest site in Huntington County. Beginning in 1972, the building that housed the press fell into disrepair and the unit sat unused.

In 1991 the Amos Schwartz Construction Company dismantled, restored, and reassembled the press in the Swiss Heritage Village in Adams County, where it now churns out delicious apple cider for the annual Berne Heritage Festival. The barn was also restored using much of the original timber, furthering the feel of nineteenth-century America.

You can see the press and enjoy the festival at the Swiss Heritage Village in September each year. The village is open May to October with fifteen restored buildings re-creating life in Adams County at the turn of the century—not this past one, but 200 years ago. Trained docents guide visitors through the village, where they may meet a variety of living-history interpreters going about their day-to-day activities as if you'd come to call in 1900.

If you like Conner Prairie in Indy, you'll love this place. Call for more info at (260) 589–8007. Berne is at the junction of U.S. 27 and SR 218.

At right:
The wrench barn in Bryant.
We were afraid to ask why.

ONE GOOD TURN
Bryant

Ernest Murphy had a wrenching experience more than thirty years ago. For reasons that are still unclear, he decided that his barn in Bryant would look better with a few adornments. He started nailing wrenches, hundreds of them, to the barn. Not just any wrenches, but antique wrenches, Amish wrenches (whatever that means), Model T wrenches, horse and buggy wrenches. Wrenches, wrenches, wrenches.

That's all there is to this story, except the photo, in case you don't believe us. If you want to see the wrenches, just head up to Bryant by going north on U.S. 27 from I–70, out of Richmond. If you don't see the barn, ask. Everyone knows where it is. Just a warning: This place attracts all the nuts.

THE WRITE STUFF

*I*f it weren't for a drinking problem, Jim Barbieri would never have gotten a job at the News-Banner in Bluffton. It wasn't Barbieri who was drinking, but a reporter at a Chicago paper where Barbieri had been hired to stuff envelopes. Despite his hapless job, Barbieri kept insisting to his boss that he was really a reporter. So when the tipsy journalist couldn't stand for himself, Barbieri was asked to stand in for him. That was all a long time ago—over fifty years—at the Chicago American, the only other newspaper where Barbieri has ever worked. Now, a half century later, the seventy-three-year old is probably the longest continually working newspaperman in Indiana.

Since coming to the Bluffton News-Banner in 1950, Barbieri has written an average of least four stories a day, six days a week. He writes an editorial every day and a news-of-the-week-in-review on Saturday, which is easy to do, since he wrote most of the stories to begin with.

Barbieri has only missed one day of work at the paper. Even while hospitalized he filed stories and editorials. A typical workday is seventeen hours, often beginning at 1:30 A.M., and includes forty cups of coffee. Until recently, he helped with his grandson's paper route, just to keep in shape.

Indy's senior newsman, Jim Barbieri, at his desk,
where he always is, unless he's covering a story,
which he always is.

Barbieri works during lunch, talks shop during dinner, and seldom takes a vacation. He has interviewed or queried Presidents Nixon, Ford, Carter, Bush, and Clinton, even Boris Yeltsin at the Kremlin. Barbieri wears two hearing aids, but he's heard it all.

The reason we called him was to see if he knew of anything interesting in Wells County. He suggested we do a chapter on the pretzel factories in town. But after hearing Barbieri's life, we think this is a better twist on the story.

SMALL-TIME ART
Carmel

If you say that Doreen Squire Ficara is the executive director of the world's smallest children's art museum, she'll correct you. "It's not a museum, it's an art gallery," says the British-born Ficara, who is very particular about the issue.

She should be. The *Guinness Book of World Records* has deemed her establishment in Carmel the "world's smallest children's art gallery," and she's got the certificate to prove it.

The museum, I mean the gallery, is about 9 feet by 15 feet. But there can be no "abouts" about it, so a city engineer measured the gallery, just to be sure.

Each month the gallery features student artwork from different local schools. Art teachers select the pieces and design the four tiny walls. The gallery is booked at least three years in advance.

A couple thousand people visit each year, but needless to say there is a high concentration of parents and grandparents eager to see their loved ones' first "showing."

Every young exhibitor receives a certificate authenticating and confirming their work was displayed at the world's smallest children's art gallery.

Ficara had researched the issue before approaching *Guinness,* only to discover there was only one other children's art gallery in the country listed in the record book. Which means that the gallery is also the second biggest children's art gallery in the world.

The gallery is at 30 West Main in Carmel. You can call Ficara at (317) 582–1455.

WELL WISHING
Carmel

For almost one hundred years, the people of Hamilton and surrounding counties have come to 116th Street near Gray Road in Carmel to get a jug, a jar, or in some cases, a barrel of the crystal clear (usually) H_2O that gurgles out of a standing pipe within eyeshot of the main road.

Historians say the well was first discovered in 1903 while surveyors and excavators were looking for natural gas. As far back as anyone can remember, residents were convinced that the artesian water not only tasted better, but also had curative powers. Talk to people in line at the well and they'll tell you the water helps cure arthritis, eases back pain, prevents headaches, and soothes sore throats. And it tastes pretty good, too.

No one knows for sure where the water originates, though the best guess seems to be somewhere in the northeastern part of the state. "We really don't know," admits John Duffy, director of Carmel Utilities, "and that's part of the mystery, part of the charm."

The well has flowed almost continuously for a century with the exception of an unexplained slowing down in the 1960s and a complete stoppage for a while in the mid-1970s. The well attracts an estimated 5,000 people a month. Why not? It's free.

In the 1990s the immediate area became a park, and a quaint little shelter was built to protect people from the rain while they were getting their water. Huh?

During an evaluation and cleaning in 1999, complaints, uh, flowed in when the pipe was turned off. Residents, convinced that the well's water could cure even cancer, panicked when the well ran dry.

The well opened months later to long lines of thirsty residents who apparently not only drink the stuff, but also wash their hair and bathe in it. "My mother drank from it and my grandmother drank from it," said one woman, "and they both lived to be ninety. That's good enough for me."

And it's cheaper than Perrier.

ROCK CONCERT
Carmel

When John Schuler, an executive for a major aggregate company (they pulverize stone for construction), had the unenviable job of creating some positive publicity, he knew he had his work cut out for him. "Most folks don't want an eighty-acre hole in their community," notes Schuler.

As luck would have it, Schuler was also elected to the board of the symphony in Carmel, a bedroom community just north of Indianapolis. Schuler, who admits to an occasional offbeat notion, decided to combine his two missions. The result was America's first true rock concert, a full symphony orchestra playing from the very bottom of a huge limestone quarry.

Schuler admits to some skepticism by musicians and townspeople alike, but after a well-orchestrated PR campaign, he had the symphony playing his song. Musicians and patrons were bused to the bottom of the cavern, about 220 feet, where food and wine were served. Choirs sang, fireworks popped, and the symphony played. It gave a whole new meaning to orchestra pit.

The acoustics are good, it's nice and cool, and it's a great fundraiser. But in 2002 it seemed to take a geologic era for the food to reach the bottom of the quarry. Some said the food tasted good, but the service was the pits. Very funny.

Classical music in a hard rock orchestra pit—only in Carmel.

PHOTO: Martin Marietta Aggregates

Will the event continue? They're looking over the situation. You can look at the hole anytime at 1980 116th Street. Call Martin Marietta Aggregates at (317) 573–4460 for information on the next concert.

FIRED UP FOR SAFETY

*I*n the early 1990s, a group of firefighters were in search of a better way to get across some lifesaving messages to kids. "Standing up in front of kids in a tie and jacket and passing out equipment just wasn't making it," says Chad Abel of the Fishers Fire Department just outside of Indianapolis.

So in 1991 Chief Phil Kouwe, a firefighter with both a passion and a song in his heart, decided that music was the way to capture the imagination of the elementary school kids. Lucky for Kouwe, he was not the only frustrated musician in the fire department. In a flash, the station had written a series of songs like "Stop, Drop and Roll," "Don't Play with Fire," and "Smoke Detector Blues."

With some makeshift musical equipment and a mascot named Sparky (a firefighter in shag), the new group, known as M. C. Axe and the Fireboys, began visiting local schools. "It caught on like wildfire," laughs Abel, "and before you knew it, the requests just came streaming in."

Now known as M. C. Axe and the Firecrew, the Fishers Fire Department is equipped with almost state-of-the-art musical gear. With a new crew of musicians and a black Lab named Kasey, they travel Indiana and neighboring states to spread the word. Kasey actually performs some of the maneuvers, showing kids how to stop, drop, and roll during a fire. M. C. Axe and the Firecrew has reached more than a million kids and is often booked months in advance. Their newest songs, many based on popular tunes, include "The Heat is On," "Matches and Lighters" (to the tune of "Run Around Sue"), and the "Seat Belt Song" ("Me and Julio Down by the School Yard"). In addition to two CDs, they have a music video.

How long will M. C. Axe and the Firecrew continue to sing? "We're hot," laughs Abel, "and we have no intention of cooling down."

Check out their Web site at: *www.mcaxeandkasey.com.*

OUT OF THIS WORLD
Chesterfield

I t would be hard to find fifty acres in Indiana more steeped in mystery than Camp Chesterfield. For 125 years, this enclave in Madison County has been the home or the stopping place for thousands of spiritualists—men and women who believe that while life on earth may be temporary, you live forever in the spirit world—which is only a séance away.

While skeptics may mock the supernatural aspect of the camp, Chesterfield attracts thousands of visitors each year—people who hope to reestablish contact with long-lost family and friends or just learn about the psychic world. Year-round there are educational programs open to the public as well as demonstrations for curious visitors and passionate believers.

On any given day, séances are conducted throughout the grounds, always by personnel who have been personally tested by the Camp Chesterfield Board and judged to be competent in various aspects of the supernatural and spiritual world. Mediums, for example, might be tested in the area of Séances and Trances. Now that's an SAT exam.

While a visit to the grounds is free, a one-on-one consultation with a medium is charged accordingly. Whatever your thing, be it psychic phenomenon, handwriting analysis, astrology, or faith healing, there is an opportunity to take a class or have a private consultation with a staff member.

Other attractions include the large busts of the gods (Christ, Buddha, Mohammed, etc.) and the stone cave where you can pray or commune. There's also a large totem pole to celebrate the spirit world of the American Indian.

Want to stick around for a while? There's a cafeteria, a campsite area, and hotels in the neighborhood. Yes, a world of activity as well as other-world activity. To learn more, call the camp at (765) 378–0237 or see its Web site: www. Campchesterfield.net.

S HE L L - S HOCKED
C h u r u b u s c o

They call it Turtle Town, this tiny village just 20 miles northwest of Fort Wayne. It has a rich history and its own version of the Loch Ness monster. Even the town name is steeped in folklore. A century and a half ago, local residents sparred over what to name their city. A fuzzy history says the name came from a city in Mexico where the Americans had waged a successful battle in the war with that country. Regardless, myth has it that even the people who picked the name had trouble pronouncing it.

Despite the tongue-twister name, Churubusco residents take great pride in their city, and they bask in the myth of the giant turtle that put their town on the map. The turtle was first sighted in 1898 in a lake belonging to one Oscar Fulk. Fifty years later, in 1948, when local farmer Gale Harris owned the lake, he claimed a similar sighting. Soon reporters and news cameras infiltrated Churubusco. Harris even drained much of the pond in search of Oscar (named after the turtle's original "founder"), but no luck.

How big was he? Some say as big as a tabletop (but people have different ideas of how big a table is); others say at least 500 pounds. Still others scoff at the notion that such a turtle ever existed. The skeptics are usually from Fort Wayne. A few people in Churubusco still claim to have seen Oscar, also dubbed the "Beast of Busco," but these people are usually drinking a Budweiser and winking at you.

Oscar and Churubusco will always be linked. And every June for the past twenty-five years, this town has honored its hard-bodied friend with four days of music, dancing, turtle contests, food, laughter, and a parade.

Churubusco is easy to find. Just head north on U.S. 33, about twenty minutes out of Fort Wayne. No rush. Everyone is on turtle time. I'd go in June. Not a heck of a lot going on otherwise.

MULTI-FACETED JAY COUNTY
Dunkirk

The slogan for Dunkirk should be: Eat Here, Get Gas. And Glass. This tiny town in Jay County was considered by many to have been the glass and gas capital of the world—and in some ways it still is.

The city's population peaked in the 1890s because natural gas was free. Yes, free. A geological dome in the area actually trapped the precious substance, making it so plentiful that glass producers flocked to the Dunkirk area for the gas they needed for manufacturing purposes. At the turn of the century, there were more than a hundred local glass manufacturers in east central Indiana; a handful still remain, with two still operating in Dunkirk: Indiana Glass and St. Gobain.

But the town's big attraction is the Glass Museum, a two-story building filled with 6,000 pieces of glassware from 110 factories (past and present). Glistening from cases are leaded lamps, glass canes, chandeliers, bowls, bottles, stemware,

vases, and candlesticks. Glass specifically from the Great
Depression is of special historical significance because of its
beauty and rarity. And of course, the big favorites are pieces
made by the Indiana Glass Company, still firing away just minutes from the museum.

Curator Mary Newsome is especially proud of the Vaseline
glass, produced by Albany Glass, in a factory that burned down
in 1929. Another favorite: a set of candlesticks surrounded by
crystals worth about $10,000. And there's a Belgian glass bas-
ket made with one piece of glass. "I'm not sure what it's worth,
but it's the only thing that the last curator ever locked up during the winter," says Newsome.

Visitors from all over the world come to the Glass Museum,
15 miles northeast of Muncie on SR 167 (765–768–6872). The
museum's hours are 10:00 A.M. to 4:00 P.M. Tuesday through
Saturday, and Sunday by appointment. If you don't love the
place, keep it to yourself. You know what they say about people
in glass houses.

RECREATIONAL TREKS
Elkhart

Question: When is a museum not a museum?
Answer: When it's a filing cabinet.

That might be a bit of an exaggeration, but Carl Ehry,
president of the Recreational Vehicle/Manufactured Housing
Museum, confesses his museum was pretty much that up until
ten years ago.

From 1972 until 1990, historical information about RVs and
manufactured homes was archived in Washington, D.C. Then a
group of suppliers, dealers, and manufacturers pushed for a

real home in Elkhart, which is home to more than one hundred RV and MH manufacturers, including Coachmen, Jayco, Monaco, Holiday Rambler, Carriage, Skyline, Patriot, Liberty, and Fairmont. At one time, half of all recreational vehicles on the road came from the Elkhart area.

The 20,000-square-foot RV/MH Heritage Foundation head-quarters is dedicated to preserving the history of the industry, celebrating the positive aspects of the lifestyle, and honoring the people who have made lasting and creative contributions to recreational vehicling (which isn't a word, so don't look it up).

The history of recreational vehicles! Only in Indiana could you get credit for that course.

Inside the Hall of Fame Museum, you can saunter through a parklike setting among the twenty-five vehicles representing the history of RVs. You'll see a 1913 RV, possibly the oldest still in existence, as well as the first Coachmen and an early Winnebago. Also displayed are 225 portraits of pioneers and inventors who made lasting contributions to the industry, as well as artifacts and memorabilia going back more than eighty-five years. Like to read? You can peruse the 10,000 volumes of RV research, magazines, newsletters, and manufacturers' catalogs. We'd rather go to the snack bar.

The museum, at 801 Benham Avenue in Elkhart, is open 9:00 A.M. to 5:00 P.M., Monday–Friday, and from 10 A.M. to 3:00 P.M. on Saturdays in June, July, and August. Need a place to stay? There are hotels, but most people who dig this stuff already have a place to sleep. Call (800) 378–8694 or check out its Web site: www.rv-mh-hall-of-fame.org.

INFLUENCE OF SPHERE
Elwood

If you wander into the Spencer Lapidary (at the intersection of State Roads 13 and 37 in Elwood) and Glen Spencer isn't there, take a peek in the back room. If you didn't know better, you'd swear you walked into the laboratory of a mad scientist.

But Glen Edwin Spencer is not crazy, just mad about rocks. It doesn't matter the size or shape. When he is through with them, they will be spheres—perfectly round balls. "We put bowling balls to shame," says Spencer.

His fascination began more than forty years ago when he and his brother, Orville (how can an idea not fly when your brother is named Orville?), were collecting rocks in Oregon.

Round and round! Glen Spencer is Elwood's
smoothest operator.

Returning to Indiana, Spencer decided he wanted to turn those
rocks into decorative globes. But how to do it?

Using his background as an electrician, he masterminded,
created, and rigged equipment to grind and polish jagged
pieces of beautiful rock into priceless, perfectly round works of
art. The machinery looks almost like a Rube Goldberg arrange-
ment and the result is a process that has fascinated people for
thirty years. Gotta see it. Can't explain it.

So unique are his machines and his methods that he is now
recognized as one of the master sphere cutters in the United
States. The Fermi Atomic Laboratory in Chicago asked Spencer

to make a machine that could produce perfect spheres for research into the origin of the earth. Mission accomplished.

Spencer claims he can make a sphere out of almost any kind of rock, but the polished luster that attracts customers is difficult to create unless the stone is dense. His favorites include obsidian and septarian nodule. But you probably knew that.

And who would want these spheres? People who just enjoy their beauty or those who believe, as did the Greeks, that spheres have a magical power. Whatever your reason, be prepared to pay anywhere from fifty bucks all the way to $5,000. Those are just round numbers, of course.

Spencer is almost always there, but call first because if he's in the back, he won't hear you; (765) 552–0784.

S A L T   O F   T H E   E A R T H
F o r t   W a y n e

Myrtle Young loves potato chips. She doesn't eat them though. She collects them. "I have more than 400," says the seventy-seven-year-old Fort Wayne native. "I have hearts, butterflies, cartoon characters, and many profiles of famous people."

No, she hasn't been sniffing snack fumes. Other people can see the resemblances, too. In fact, her lauded collection—the only known one in the world—has taken her around the globe.

Late-night television fans may remember Young's 1987 appearance with Johnny Carson. As she was showing off her chips, a loud crunch was heard. Had Johnny eaten one of her prized chips? Young grasped her chest, shocked that Johnny would do such a dastardly deed.

Johnny then revealed a bowl of chips he had stashed under his desk. *TV Guide* voted this classic Carson gag as television's funniest moment. "The editors of *TV Guide* told me that I was

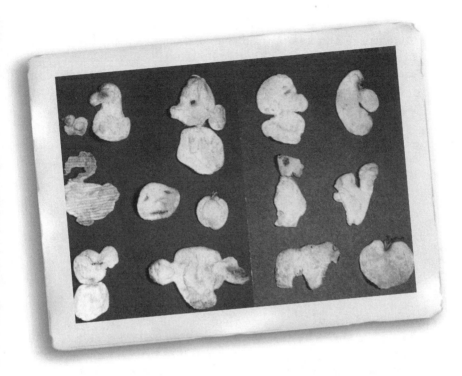

Betcha can't eat just one. But stop! These chips are priceless.
PHOTO: Myrtle Young

in the top fifty," says Young. "When I bought the issue, I just kept turning the pages and turning the pages to find out where I was listed. I was surprised to see that Johnny and I were number one."

Young has chips that look like George Bush, Rodney Dangerfield, Yogi Bear, and Snoopy. But her most famous chip has an uncanny resemblance to Bob Hope. When word got back to Hope about the caricature chip, he sent an autographed picture to Young signed, "So you'll remember what I really look like. Keep chipping away."

And she has. Young has displayed her collection in Bali, Japan, Hong Kong, and London. The chips always travel first class—packed in cotton batting and always in carry-on luggage.

They have been viewed by international television audiences, Princess Diana, and the Queen of England. Such acclaim has prompted the Indianapolis Children's Museum, *Ripley's Believe It or Not,* and the Smithsonian to express interest in purchasing her collection.

Young plans to pass on her collection to her children—chips off the old block.

You can't visit Young, but buy an old video of "The Tonight Show" and you'll see her.

Buffalo Things
Fremont

Heard of buffalo? Sure you've heard of buffalo. But what about a buffalo herd, 300 of them, right here in Indiana? Just roam over to Fremont, in Steuben County, and you'll find the third largest private herd in North America and the largest in the state. The preserve, opened in 2001, was the dream of Dr. John Trippy, an Ohio-based surgeon whose visit to Yellowstone National Park as a small boy made a huge impression. Trippy opened the park to "honor and preserve the land, the buffalo, and the people." Combine the buffalo herd with a bed-and-breakfast and a gift shop and you have all the makings of a unique attraction.

Visitors to the preserve—whether they opt for the bed-and-breakfast or not—are taken on a truck tour that allows up-close viewing of the buffalo. "People are not allowed out of the truck," says Misty Smith, the preserve manager. "These are wild animals and they weigh up to 2,500 pounds. You wouldn't want one to go after you."

Along with the tour comes a brief lesson on the impact of the buffalo on American history. The gift shop sells Native

American jewelry, buffalo hides, head mounts, and knives, as well as books and tapes further recounting the story of the American bison.

Those who purchase the overnight package can enjoy a buffalo breakfast, which includes buffalo sausage or a buffalo casserole. Those with heftier appetites can hold out for the buffalo steak for dinner, which is less fatty and more nutritious. Or am I confusing this with ostrich?

The buffalo meat is fresh because male buffaloes on the preserve are slaughtered, then butchered on site. And the meat can be bought frozen in the gift shop. The Wild Winds Buffalo Preserve is located next to the Indiana Turnpike in the heart of the tri-state area bordered by Michigan and Ohio. Call (260) 495–0137 for more information and exact directions.

LIMBERLOST
Geneva

Why would anyone want to take farmland and turn it into a swamp? Ask Ken Brunswick, a man whose mission is to do just that. Brunswick and his associates want to re-create the historical setting of one of America's most successful authors, Gene Stratton-Porter.

Geneva Grace Stratton, born in Wabash County in 1863, moved to Adams County with her husband in 1886. Here they built a more-than-modest fourteen-room Queen Anne home, where Mrs. Stratton-Porter wrote many of her novels and poems. Eight of her books ultimately became motion pictures.

Her inspiration? The nearby Limberlost Swamp, once described as a "treacherous swamp, quagmire, filled with every plant, animal, and human danger known." But Stratton-Porter, who prided herself as a naturalist, wanted to instill her love of

Mrs. Stratton-Porter lived near a swamp
only a writer could love.

PHOTO: Indiana State Museum

the earth in her writing. And she just loved that swamp, like only a mother could.

By 1913 the swamp was ditched and drained. Stratton-Porter moved to northern Indiana where she built another home near Rome City (Noble County), known as Wildflower Woods. Visitors marvel at the two-story cabin with exterior cedar logs, the magnificent fireplaces, and furnishings and memorabilia belonging to the Porters.

But back to Geneva, where hundreds of acres of that original swamp are in the process of being restored. Visitors with a love of literature and the wild can hike the area and see mallard ducks, bald eagles, sandhill cranes, and tundra swans, all the result of restoring the swamp. Brunswick, who started the project eight years ago, is removing the hundred-year-old drainage hardware. "When they began this in 1888, they said they were reclaiming the land. But they never had it to begin with."

Whichever Stratton-Porter historical site you visit, you'll enjoy a walk back in time. But many prefer her first home next to Limberlost. Let's just say it's a "swamp thing."

Limberlost is located at 200 East Sixth, one block east of U.S. 27 in Geneva. The home is closed Mondays and Tuesdays and from mid-December through March. Call (260) 368–7428 for exact times. The Rome City home is northwest of Fort Wayne, just north of U.S. 6 on State Road 9 (1205 Pleasant Point).

BURSTING WITH PRIDE

*H*untington County is not embarrassed by the fact that its most famous resident was a total bubble brain. Eiffel Plasterer had a passion for ordinary and not-so-ordinary soap bubbles, and he fascinated children and adults with his demonstrations for almost a century.

Plasterer was a man of both religion and science, a bit of a conflict in the 1920s when he attended DePauw University. Here he became especially intrigued with bubbles and began working on the perfect bubble solution (a concoction of liquid soap, water, and glycerine) as part of a lifelong attempt to produce an almost unbreakable bubble.

Plasterer blew bubbles at schools, church meetings, conventions, and banquets and on street corners. He wrote scientific articles and lectured in schools and universities, all the time blowing his own exquisite bubbles. Bubbles within bubbles, bubbles on top of bubbles, bubbles, bubbles, bubbles.

And he blew those bubbles on more TV shows than you could shake a wand at: Letterman, Tom Snyder, and Dick Cavett. Plasterer also holds the record for bubble longevity, capturing a bubble inside a mason jar to protect it from air currents and keeping it intact for one day short of a year. Longer than most gerbils live.

Plasterer believed you never outgrew the joy you could get by blowing bubbles, and he preached that philosophy up until he was almost ninety. Eiffel Lane, named after the famous bubbleologist, now runs through Hiers Park in Huntington. Plasterer's words still ring loud and clear as a bubble. "Our hopes and dreams are the bubbles of life we are blowing. They do not all have to break."

Eiffel Plasterer: all dressed up with someplace to blow.

PHOTO: Alice Stickler

VICE SQUAD
Huntington

I t's a museum for politicians. But they claim to be nonprofit and nonpartisan. Already the whole thing seems a little suspicious. But it's true. The Dan Quayle Center is the only vice presidential museum in America. It started out in 1993 just honoring Dan Quayle, but Quayle himself was uncomfortable with the sole spotlight and encouraged the board to turn the old Christian Science building into an educational facility featuring all the number twos. It has paid off. The museum greets thousands of school kids each year.

Indiana claims five vice presidents and three also-rans and is second only to New York in the number of native-born veeps. And so—being second to New York—the Hoosier State is the perfect place for a shrine to seconds. The museum has artifacts representing all forty-six vice presidents, as well political buttons, political cartoons, books, and other memorabilia.

But Quayle does have the most space in the museum, an entire floor all to himself. In the display you can see everything from his report card to his dog-chewed high school diploma. There's a letter that the vice president wrote to his father during the 1989 invasion of Panama and a photo of James Danforth, the World War II soldier killed in action for whom Quayle was named. An entire section is devoted to newspaper and TV coverage of Quayle and the sometimes unfair treatment by the press. One display details the Murphy Brown speech and the ensuing media blitz.

The museum is at 815 Warren Street in Huntington, just minutes from where Quayle grew up and right across the street from the elementary school where he learned to spell potato . . . or potatoe. Whatever.

The museum is open Tuesday through Saturday 10:00 A.M. to 4:00 P.M. and Sunday, 1:00 to 4:00 P.M. Information is available at (260) 356–6356 or www.quaylemuseum.org.

MILLING AROUND
Kendallville

The windmill museum in Kendallville, Indiana, may be the only one of its kind in the United States. But it's the perfect place for it. According to Russell Baker, president of the local historical society, seventy-eight windmill companies surrounded Kendallville in the early 1900s.

Baker started the project a few years ago to create a tourist attraction in Noble County. His interest was further piqued when he discovered that his own great-grandfather was a windmill builder. The mills, constructed to pump water, were built on-site following the digging of the well.

Baker and his associates purchased some land and then refurbished a barn for use as a museum. Before long the museum founders brought in old windmills from all over the country, restored them, and put them on the museum grounds. One, a replica of the first windmill in North America, is known as the Robertson Windmill. The original was brought from England and erected on the James River in Virginia.

With more than fifty windmills on the museum grounds, and plans for another fifty or so to come, the Mid-America Windmill Museum is unique in its mission to educate people on the history of wind power. Windmills here rise as high as 55 feet, although most are in the 25-foot range. All the windmills work, and a handful are connected to underground wells.

Russell Baker and his windmills. One good turn deserves another.

Inside the museum, patrons can see old photographs, models, and exhibits. A nine-minute video tells the history of wind power from the Persians (around A.D. 300) through modern times and hydroelectric power. The last weekend in June is festival time, celebrated with historic windmill exhibits. As a highlight, museum employees drill a well, erect a windmill, and by the end of the weekend it is pumping water.

Admission is free, but the museum is open only during the summer from Memorial Day through Labor Day. Kendallville is on U.S. 6 about a half hour northwest of Fort Wayne. You can reach Russell Baker at (260) 347–0875 or try the Web site, www.midamericawindmillmuseum.com. When we were there, most locals had no idea how to find the place. So just keep looking. Up.

WILLOW, NOT WICKER
Lapel

G reg Adams doesn't claim to be the only willow artisan in the Midwest, but he may be the only one crazy enough to open an entire shop selling willow furniture. "Most willow guys just mess around in their garage," says Adams, "but I figured I'd do it right."

Adams, a social worker by day, spends his weekends in the 1,500-square-foot studio (a former grocery store from the 1890s) where he caters to a largely urban clientele looking for a rustic touch in their homes. He displays several dozen pieces that range from a simple wreath for a couple of bucks to a majestic, canopy willow bed that you can get into (and under) for $600.

His willow mania began on a fishing trip almost twenty years ago when he couldn't catch any fish, but his imagination captured something else. Surrounded by willow branch saplings, Adams wondered if he could make baskets like the Indians. Through trial and error, he branched out and taught himself to make wreaths, trellises, arbors, headboards, plant stands, and screens. Walk into his shop and you feel like you're in a tropical rain forest. Oh, and it smells so good.

Thank you for shopping at Adams Willow shop.
You're willcome.

Adams has another passion: He travels the rural highways
of Indiana looking for . . . well, he's not sure what he's looking
for. "I'm a student of the back roads. I get in my car and just
drive. I like finding roads that I've never seen before. In the
process, I'll be scouting for some willows."

His shop sits on the main drag of Lapel. Take State Road 37
from Indianapolis to Highway 32, then east to State Road 13,
then turn right and go 5 blocks to Main Street. He's open on
weekends, but call first to make sure he's not out driving
around: (765) 534–3009. You can also make an appointment.
By the way, Adams hates the word wicker. He likes the word
willow. You don't want to make that mistake with so many
wickets around.

DUMPLINGS WITHOUT A PEEL
Lapel

G len Grabow is an engineer. He's got a degree from Marquette University. He worked on the Polaris Missile and the Hubble Telescope. This is big stuff. Now he makes apple dumplings for a living. He's never been happier.

When Grabow retired in 1989, he bought an apple orchard in Madison County and decided to add a small bakery to the operation. His apple dumplings had gained a bit of a local reputation over the years, so when the Food Channel was looking for a feature segment on orchard/bakery combos, they picked Grabow's.

The segment aired in January of 2001 and things haven't been the same since. "I answered the phones and took orders for ten straight hours," says Grabow, whose success created a major problem: How do you ship a product like this and keep it flaky and tasty?

Grabow looked at it like any good engineer and created a "kit," which could be sent to hungry customers. Inside the box, dumpling lovers will find the uncooked dumpling, along with special sauce, glaze, instructions, and a comment card. We hope McDonald's doesn't steal this idea. The secret to these dumplings is, well, it's a secret. But if you want to try dumplings at home, Grabow strongly advises coring, peeling, and slicing the apple. "And keep the crust thin," he says.

You can buy the dumplings fresh at his orchard bakery for a couple of bucks each by taking I–69 to exit 14, which is State Road 13. Turn left toward Lapel, travel 1 mile, and look on the left. Call if you get lost: (888) 534–3225. If you want to send dumplings to your sister in Denver, you're talking seven dollars each. And she has to bake them herself. Only Glen Grabow could have engineered that.

NOBLE MUSEUM
Ligonier

B ored with your DVD? You might want to hearken back to
the days when you could just get into your BVDs and listen
to the radio. No better place to hearken than Ligonier, Indiana.

When the Indiana Radio Historical Society was founded in
1972, its first display was atop the Auburn Car Museum. But
an old filling station in Ligonier caught its eye and soon
became one of the few freestanding museums in the country
dedicated to the history of radio.

Inside the museum, thousands of visitors each year see
about 400 radios, a few dating back to 1899. Each radio is
tagged with a bit of history. Also displayed are vacuum tubes
invented in 1906, still in their original boxes. You can see novelty radios in the shapes of food products, as well as radios
used during wartime. Also inside are cathedral and tombstone
radios, telegraphy, crystal sets, and horn and cone speakers.

The museum has a small transmitter that plays radio shows,
and museum-goers can actually fiddle with an old-time radio
dial to simulate how listeners from the 1920s and '30s tuned in
their favorite shows. Kids especially enjoy the old-time tele-
graph keys or making their hair stand on end with a Van der
Graaf generator.

The museum is open May through October, Tuesday through
Saturday from 10:00 A.M. to 3:00 P.M. From November through
April it's open on Saturdays, from 10:00 A.M. to 2:00 P.M. It's
right off the main drag in Ligonier, but call if you're lost: (888)
417–3562.

*B*EAT THE *C*LUCK
Mentone

You probably don't know this—or care—but there is a raging controversy over where the world's largest egg is. Neither side has cracked; both maintain they harbor the biggest. The folks in Winlock, Washington, have one that's 12 feet long and 1,200 pounds; it sits on a steel pedestal, atop a pole. The sign next to it says: World's Largest Egg.

But Hoosiers disagree! In Mentone, Indiana (Kosciusko County), sits an even bigger egg—maybe. This egg weighs 3,000 pounds and is 10 feet high, so it's definitely heavier. But is it bigger?

Kosciuskoans (if there is such a word) say, YES! Mentonians agree. Mentone has been a center of egg production for over a hundred years. By the turn of the nineteenth century, Mentone chicken farmers were bringing their eggs by covered wagon to the train station for delivery throughout the Midwest. There were even judges who assessed the relative eggyness of the farmers' products.

Three huge egg producers still ship from Mentone, a city with far more chickens than people. Their annual Egg Festival in June celebrates their rich egg history with music, food, a parade, a 5K run and, of course, an egg toss. There's also a group of performers called the Hen House Five. Fortunately we have no photo of this.

But the real excitement is the big Chicken Drop event. Chickens are placed in cages where the floor is marked with a series of numbers. Then the audience places bets on where . . . you know. I don't think we really need to explain this.

Mentone is on State Road 25, southwest of Warsaw. The Egg Festival is usually the first weekend after the first of June, but call the Kosciusko Convention & Visitors Bureau at (574) 269–6090 to check. Sometimes it isn't.

THAT'S DAFFY
Milford

Indiana is the largest exporter of duck feet in the United States. And you thought we were just proud of our racetrack.

Duck feet, it turns out (and they do turn out), are considered a delicacy in the Far East. These very chewy fowl entrees are typically boiled before serving. The cartilage, however, is eschewed—as opposed to chewed. Duck feet are included on dim sum carts with a side of black bean sauce. I don't know about you, but my mouth is already watering.

Another popular duck dish is *czarnina,* a traditional sweet Polish soup also known as duck blood soup. It's usually made with prunes, raisins, dried fruit, and noodles or dumplings. The concoction is then thickened with flour and fresh duck blood. Always a hit with guests during the holidays.

To learn more fabulous fowl facts, check out Maple Leaf Farms' Duck University (www.mapleleaffarms.com). The farm is headquartered in Milford and is one of seven U.S. companies that process ducks. And it seems the creation of D. U. ("Lean to the front, lean to the back, stand up, sit down, quack, quack, quack!") was to inform the masses of the benefits of duck consumption. This agricultural institute of higher learning is "dedicated to fostering a deeper understanding for duckling."

Maple Leaf Farms also supplies many restaurants and caterers with duck legs and assorted parts. There's also a big demand for duck feathers for pillows, comforters, and down clothing. Milford is 43 miles southeast of South Bend, just south of State Road 6 and State Road 15. Call first: (574) 658–4121. Are you really going?

By the way, people in Asia, where they eat the entire duck, have some advice: Always eat the feet last, so you don't end up with the bill. (Sorry!)

STANDING ROOM ONLY
Montpelier

The 60-foot fiberglass Indian chief that sits (well, stands) in the middle of tiny Montpelier can be seen by everybody—no reservation required. Montpelier, a city that boasts a rich and somewhat saucy history of murder, brothels, and drinking, has calmed down quite a bit in the last hundred years. But the mammoth presence of Chief Francois Godfroy, the last war chief of the Miamis, is a pretty good reminder of the rich Indiana heritage in Blackford County.

The statue was originally located at a Pontiac dealership in Indy, then moved to the Turtle Creek Museum.

Downtown Montpelier. Apparently more effective than a stop sign.

They were going to ship the Indian to the new Eiteljorg
Museum in 1985. When those plans were nixed, the chief's
great-great-grandson Larry (how many Indians do you know
named Larry?) arranged for Montpelier to display the icon in
the center of town, provided that the statue would be placed at
the entrance to any future park in the city.

So far, no park. In the meantime the chief keeps watch over
the city's quaint shops. Or should we say paint. The stores are
actually painted on stone walls, the kind of busy main street
that might have existed in another place or time. Ken Neff, former mayor, had seen the concept in his travels and brought the
idea back to Montpelier where a local artist sketched in the outline and volunteers then painted by number.

It's not real estate, it's fake estate, although all the stores
represented, like Neff Realty, Neff Insurance, Walker Glancy
Funeral Home, Grandma's Joes, and Frosty's, really exist in the
city, but are somewhat less idyllic in real life.

Montpelier is on Highway 18, just west of where it intersects
with Highway 1, about a half hour east of Marion.

PUTTING A LID ON IT
Muncie

Rev. Philip Robinson can't keep a lid on his enthusiasm. But
he can keep lids on some 4,000 fruit and canning jars in his
museum in Muncie.

It was a single lid, in fact, that Robinson found thirty-one
years ago while cleaning up an abandoned lot that led him to
create his nationally known collection. He became intrigued
with the abandoned top, curious to know what kind of a jar it
came from. After years of searching, he finally located the lid's

A jarring thought: Reverend Robinson may have the biggest collection of jars in the world.

mate at a flea market. Both the lid and the glass container said "Hoosier Jar." The glass jar, he learned, was made in Greenfield, Indiana, in 1882. Robinson paid $700 for the jar. He could have sold the lid for $100.

In Robinson's museum, a building just outside his home, the jars are arranged in a very scientific manner. "If it fits on the shelf, that's where I put it," says Robinson, who has jars as old as 1849 and as new as "just made yesterday." He's got jars from scores of foreign countries and in dozens of different colors. And if the jar lid is missing or broken, he makes a new lid—just like the original—down in his workshop.

Robinson's attitude toward some of his priceless possessions is, well, priceless. He encourages people to pick up the jars, touch them, feel them, enjoy them. "If one breaks, it breaks," he says. "I lived without them before, I can survive without them now. And they're all paid for." He even feels that way about his most valuable collectible, a nameless $7,000 jar. "If you start to worry about whether it's going to break, it's no fun anymore."

No charge to see the jars. Just stop by 1201 West Cowing Drive in Muncie, but call first: (765) 282-9707. Robinson wanted me to know that his wife is the president of the National Jelly Jar Collectors. And now you know, too.

MODEL ACADEMY
Muncie

"The world headquarters for model aviation is in Muncie, Indiana!"

This proclamation can be found on the Academy of Model Aeronautics/National Model Aviation Museum's Web site (www.modelaircraft.org). It sounds like they surprised even themselves.

The AMA is the world's largest sport aviation organization with more than 17,000 members, including former astronaut Neil Armstrong. The organization sanctions more than 1,000 model competitions annually and hosts the National Aeromodeling Championships.

The museum has a full-scale version of Lindbergh's beautiful bird on display. "Visitors are amazed by the plane's detail and that this plane could fly," says Michael Smith, National Model Aviation Museum curator. "However, the planes are retired from flying once they're donated to the museum." Other models include a feather helicopter built in 1796 and a glider constructed in 1804. There are also early radio-controlled planes from the 1920s and '30s with bulky controllers that look as if enthusiasts needed to have engineering degrees to operate them.

Outside at the flying field visitors can witness some amazing acrobatics and aerial maneuvers. "We hold about thirteen competitions here each year," says Smith. "They range from dogfights to pylon races and from aircraft carrier landings to parachute contests." That's right—radio-controlled, parasail-wearing G.I. Joes jumping from RC planes and guided down toward a target. Amazing!

The aviation museum is located in Muncie at 5151 East Memorial Drive. Call (800) 435–9262 or visit www.modelaircraft.org.

Pie R Round, and Huge
Nappanee

R on Telschow, owner of Ron's Lovin' Oven in Elkhart County, will not swear he makes the biggest apple pie in the world, but we don't have the time to call every bakery. So here's the recipe:

326 pounds of apples
94 pounds of pie crust
(the rest is a secret)

Just like 1,000 mamas used to make: the world's largest apple pie.

PHOTO: Elkhart County Convention Bureau

Telschow started creating his gargantuan pies more than twenty-five years ago for the Nappanee Apple Festival. With the help of a 7-foot specially made pastry tin, he bakes the pie in a huge Reel oven (that turns like a Ferris wheel) in about two hours.

But the pie takes almost eight hours to cool before he can send it to hungry patrons at the Apple Festival, who gobble up the 800 pieces in just a few hours. While waiting, there's an apple-peeling contest, baking contest, pie-eating contest, bed races, and a crosscut saw competition. There's also a classic car rally, an antique firetruck show, and a parade with floats—and some of the floats don't even have apples. And there's no charge for any of this.

But back to that pie . . . Is it the biggest pie in the world? "I think that *Guinness* said so," says Telschow, "but I've never really checked. I could make it bigger, but I'd need a bigger oven."

To get a piece of the action and a piece of the pie, take U.S. 31 north from Indy to U.S. 6. Then U.S. 6 east into Nappanee. You can also call (800) 860–5957 for more information. By the way, Telschow claims the pie is not just big in size, but big in taste, noting that many folks say that their grandmother's apple pie just doesn't stack up to his.

DUCK, DUCK, SPRUCE
Noblesville

It looks like a duck; it walks like a duck; it quacks like a duck. But it may not be a duck. It may be a Bundy Decoy, probably the finest decorative duck decoys in the United States. And made in Indiana, just north of Noblesville.

He's not just carving decoys. They're works of art. Same price.

Okay, they don't walk and quack, but they are realistic enough that John Bundy sells a bunch (flock?) to nature lovers and even some to hunters. But Bundy Decoys are largely for show, and quite a show they make.

Bundy purchased a few unfinished decoy ducks back in the 1970s and painted them, discovering that by using the natural grain of the wood he could create unique and beautiful designs. Soon he was duck-hooked.

Bundy purchased a spindle carver so that he could craft about twelve duck bodies at a time by guiding the rotary spindles along the blocks of wood. The ninety-minute process takes great touch and feel. One mistake is twelve mistakes and a great deal of wasted timber. Then his wife, Valerie, in a process labeled top secret, paints each duck by hand. The Bundys turn out 4,000 collector ducks a year, each one different, each one sold and certified for posterity.

Bundy's tiny showroom, at 1605 Strawtown Avenue in Noblesville, is not easy to find, but if you want to see the finest hand-painted decoys this side of Lake Michigan, it's worth the waddle. It's open 9:00 A.M. to 4:00 P.M. Monday through Friday. Call for directions (800–387–3831), or visit the Web site: www.Bundyducks.com.

JUMP START
Orestes

Rob Williams is a frogmeister and a postmaster. He performs both duties in the tiny town of Orestes. And he's awful proud of both those titles. Williams oversees the annual frog-jumping contest, the only sanctioned such event east of the Mississippi.

Every June scores of people arrive for the festivities, either "renting" or bringing their own bullfrogs for the big competition. Winners of the Orestes jump-off are automatically entered in the international championships in Calaveras County, California, a contest after which Mark Twain named his famous short story. The winner there can take home five grand. The losers get green with envy.

Contestants have thirty seconds to nudge their entries into the hopping mode, then judges record the total of three jumps. "If your frog goes backwards, you're just out of luck," says Williams, who takes his frogmeistership very seriously. Winning frogs usually manage to hop about 20 feet. "We've lost a few," he adds, "but trained frog wranglers scoop up the frisky escapees."

Participants range in age from eight to eighty (people, not frogs), and kids too squeamish to handle their own frogs can enlist the help of frog jockeys to place the feisty contestants into position.

The contest is every June. Call (765) 754–8755 for more info. Orestes is just west of Alexandria on State Road 28. But get a jump on it, the place is hopping.

GIANT SAVINGS
Pendleton

Vic Cook has no desire to live like a pioneer, or a groundhog for that matter, but for almost twenty years this high school teacher and musician has lived underground. He's no hermit. In fact, his home is open to the public. You may feel his home is beneath you, but it's worth lowering yourself—about 22 feet.

It all started in the late 1970s when Cook bought some land and began work on his vision. He wanted a home that was environmentally loving (friendly is not a strong enough word), but at the same time very high-tech. He wanted to blend science, art, and nature. The house was completed in the early 1980s and opened to the public in 1986.

The underground fortress, known as The Giant, was built with Cook's own hands, using fallen trees and a backhoe. The house has seven levels and uses the energy from the surrounding woodland, energy from the sun, and geothermal energy from the earth. Cook spends not a penny on public utilities, but he can chill a beer in his hollowed-out beech tree refrigerator faster than an Amana. The secret: special insulation and underground air currents.

Thousands of students visit the 7,000-square-foot home each year after a thirty-minute trek through the surrounding forest, led by Sue Blakely, president of Cook's foundation. Inside, guests marvel at a high-tech music studio, a big-screen TV, two computers, and a washing machine. Cook runs it all for less than a buck a day, powered by six storage batteries charged by solar panels, with a back-up gasoline generator. His toilet is a composting unit, which is probably more info than you wanted, but that's what all the kids ask.

You can visit The Giant by reservation only. For more information, call (765) 778–2757 or check out the Web site: www.giantearthship.com.

In a Pinch
Pinch

The town of Pinch has no city hall. It has no downtown. Or uptown. Suburban sprawl would be putting up its first traffic light or constructing a second home. There goes the neighborhood!

Two out of three people in Pinch are Tom and Shirley.

PHOTO: Tom Fisher

Welcome to Pinch—the Hoosier State's smallest town. Its population of three suits Shirley Fisher just fine. That's because the two other residents live with her, and she's the town's self-appointed mayor. "I'm the mayor because I was born on this corner," she says with a laugh. "My husband, Tom, is second in command and my son, well, he works just beyond the city limits so I don't know what his title would be." We'd suggest "outsider."

The triumvirate—and the entire town, for that matter—can be found in Randolph County at the intersection of 900 West and 400 South. There are three buildings: an abandoned seed/feed store, Shirley's ceramic shop, and the Fishers' home. And since the city limit signs are planted in their front yard, the Fishers can take an out-of-town trip by simply climbing over their fence.

Pinch hasn't always been this small. In the late 1800s, the town was called Good View and bustled with an estimated population of twelve. The boom years ended, though, when the railroad bypassed the town, slowly derailing the population and inspiring a name change. "The story I heard is that everyone in town pinched their pennies," says Shirley. And the name has stuck ever since.

The tiniest town has had its share of media attention. Newspaper reporters, TV hosts, and even a New York fashion magazine stopped by for a spell. That just goes to show you that everyone needs a little Pinch now and then.

Pinch is located 22 miles northeast of New Castle. You can't miss it. Yeah, right.

UNIFORM APPROACH
Portland

O ld soldiers never die, they just go to the Museum of the Soldier in Portland, one of the only museums in the entire country dedicated not to the artifacts of war, but the people behind them. One of the founders, Jim Waechter, has been a collector of military history for fifty years. Brian Williamson also started at an early age. All the board members share this passion.

The museum, a former Coca Cola plant, is 26,000 square feet, and while Waechter admits he hasn't filled all the space yet, he's optimistic about the future. "We've filled about 5,000 square feet right now, and we have many collections we can use as the building expands."

What makes this museum so different is that virtually every piece of military equipment is linked to a specific person. Each item, whether donated or purchased, is accompanied by a bio and photos of the person it represents. When pieces are acquired without that information, Waechter and his volunteers become amateur sleuths, going to local and national archives, checking any available records. "It's painstaking, but our people are very good at it," he says.

For background information, unidentified trappings may be displayed in the museum, but featured items always have that personal touch. In one case, museum researchers traced a uniform based on a name scribbled on the inside pocket. The owner of the uniform was so thrilled with the discovery that he happily supplied all the accompanying material.

The museum features all wars and armed conflicts including Desert Storm, the conflict in Bosnia, and the ongoing war against terrorism. And while the displays are probably a little Hoosier-heavy because of location, the exhibit features soldiers from all over the country.

Waechter plans extensive education programs with school kids, convinced that most fathers and grandfathers talk little about their war experience. "Kids will come to the museum, not realizing their own relatives were in a particular war. We want the kids to walk out with a feeling for the person behind the rifle, of the nurse who was in the uniform, as well as those who supported us back home."

The museum is located at 516 East Arch Street in Portland. Take State Road 67 northwest from Muncie, go east on State Road 26 to Portland, then follow the signs. Call for info at (260) 726–2967.

F LEA B ITTEN
Shipshewana

We pretty much avoid the major, well-known tourist attractions in this book. And you thought you missed the chapter on the Indianapolis 500. But we'll make an exception for Shipshewana, a buggy ride back in time.

As you travel through La Grange County you will see the huge Amish population (third biggest in the country) engaged in their daily lives, the past interacting with the present. They drive horse and buggies, walk to their neighbor's instead of phoning, and get most of their food from their own farms. Then there are the Mennonites, from whom the Amish split in 1698. They have cars, E-mail, and Game Boys. You can't tell a Mennonite from an insurance salesman from Des Moines.

Now it's time to shop. Here in this tiny hamlet of Shipshewana you will find more than a thousand vendors selling every knickknack, collectible, antique, or piece of junk you can imagine. It is estimated on any given day there are more than one million completely different items for sale. Each day 30,000

people are either dallying through the market place or dicker-
ing with the clerks. This is one of the largest outdoor flea markets in the country. Can't find what you are looking for? Come
back the next day. It's there.

Once you've shopped till you dropped, try the Menno-Hof
Interpretive Center, just opposite the Shipshewana auction
grounds, where you can experience everything from a simulated tornado (Mennonites have a worldwide tornado relief mission) to a prison dungeon to see a re-creation of how the
Anabaptists (the original Mennonites) were persecuted in the
sixteenth and seventeenth centuries. You can also walk through
a seventeenth-century ship that chronicles their migration to
the United States. A total of six narrated areas all provide information about Amish and Mennonite history and lifestyle.

Okay, enough culture. Let's go shopping again.

The flea market is open on Tuesday and Wednesday, May
through October only, but great shopping can be found in town
as well. There are a number of auctions that are a hoot to just
watch. If you actually want to buy an Amish draft horse, Friday is your day. Call (260) 768–4129 for details. Shipshewana
is just north of Ligonier on State Road 5.

A-MAZING GRACE
Upland

Wouldn't it be great if there was just one place in the entire
United States where you could play a round of golf and
then walk into a labyrinth? You're kidding! You've never
thought about it before? You don't even know what a labyrinth
is? Thank goodness for this book.

A turf labyrinth is a pathway in the ground whose winding course leads inexorably to the center. Unlike a maze, there are no tricks, no cul-de-sacs, no wrong turns. This is called unicursical. Like you didn't know that. The idea is to think introspectively as you meander—instead of worrying if you can find your way out.

Labyrinths like this go back thousands of years in Europe and Asia, but they are virtually nonexistent in America. Randy and Sara Ballinger changed all that when they built a labyrinth right next to their golf course (Club Run) in Upland, Indiana. They made it to honor Randy's great-grandmother who was born near Hanover, Germany, home of one of the world's most famous turf labyrinths: The Rad, circa 1500. Randy recreated The Rad here in hope that it would generate interest in the former abolitionist community of Farmington, where his golf course now sits. Here, too, is the historic Israel Jenkins House, an important part of the Underground Railroad network in pre–Civil War Indiana.

The labyrinth is 105 feet in diameter, the paths 18 inches and the journey to the center is just over 1,400 feet. The Labyrinth opened for the millennium, and while Randy knows it is not exactly a tourist magnet, he did think that a place for meditation might sit well with golfers who wanted to prepare themselves for a good round or needed solace after a bad one.

From I–69 take exit 59 (Upland and Gas City exit), go a quarter mile east on State Road 22, then a mile north on road 700 East, then a half mile east on road 400 South to the Club Run Golf Course entrance (800–998–7651). Remember to let faster meditators pray through.

LET THERE BE LIGHT

*H*ere's a trivia question designed to stump the experts. What was the very first city to be lit by electricity? New York? Nope. Los Angeles? Sorry. Chicago? Try again.

No, the answer is Wabash. That's right, tiny Wabash in northeastern Indiana made world headlines in 1880 when four lamps were hung in the dome of the courthouse, each facing in a different direction. Powered by a threshing machine steam engine, the lights (3,000 candlepower each) were turned on at 8:00 P.M. and dazzled the city for several blocks. Most people were stunned at how far the beams reached. From this one central source, people could read their newspapers at night as far away as 6 blocks. Folks in nearby cities saw the eerie glow around Wabash.

But why Wabash? No one is quite sure, except that Wabash was clearly in the market for a cheaper way to light homes. Gas was expensive, so town leaders approached Charles Brush, inventor of the arc lamp (a lamp ignited by jumping an electric charge between two poles), who was eager to show his invention to the world. The city had a little incentive money and a courthouse on a hill, two good reasons for Brush to test his creation in Wabash. Thomas Edison, we should mention, had invented his incandescent light (made with a filament) just a few months earlier.

But Brush's lights needed constant replacing, while Edison's longer-lasting design allowed cities to light streets and homes individually. Eight years later, the Wabash Electric Light Company replaced the Brush lights with the more modern Edison equipment. In any case, Wabash was the first electrically lighted city and today's visitors to the courthouse can see one of the remaining arc lights in the lobby. A friendly janitor let me climb up (and boy, did I climb) to where the original four lamps were installed in the dome, but this area is not officially open to the public, so don't say I sent you.

To get to Wabash go fifteen minutes north of Kokomo on U.S. 31, then east on State Road 115.

ROSE-COLORED HOUSES
Wakarusa

Devon Rose is never insulted when people accuse him of thinking small. Rose, a retired draftsman, started thinking tiny in the early 1960s while working on a model railroad set with his kids. After constructing a miniature feedmill, he began whittling, shaving, and cutting, creating exact replicas of other buildings in his hometown of Wakarusa. Now, more than forty years later, Rose's life's work is displayed in his basement—arguably one of the premier miniature displays in the country.

After completing all the buildings in the Wakarusa business district, Rose then went on to replicate at least one building in each city of Elkhart County. In the past several years, he has expanded his work and now has more than 200 buildings from more than twenty-five surrounding counties.

The work is meticulous, often requiring hours and hours of painstaking attention to detail. "I got thirteen pieces of wood out of one toothpick," says Rose, "and I still threw some of the stick away." A typical building could take over 1,000 hours to complete. Rose sees no end in sight (we wonder how he can see at all), although Linda, his wife, sees the project getting too big for the basement.

Incredibly, Rose's scale is 1 inch to 5 feet, making his pieces far smaller than a typical dollhouse or miniature collection. In one part of the display, Rose has a lake stocked with tiny fish. At night, the entire project is lit with thousands of "stars." The sound of cats fighting and church music add to the realism of the work.

Rose loves to show his work, and for a nominal fee you can visit him at 325 South Elkhart Street in Wakarusa (take State Road 19 for 5 miles north of U.S. 6). Call and talk to Linda for more information: (574) 862–2367.

DYNAMITE SKATING
Westfield

TNT Hockey Academy in Westfield is dynamite. And not just because three former professional hockey players, brothers Monty, Bryan, and Rocky Trottier, run the place. It's dynamite because the ice you skate on is unreal, really. The "ice" is a plastic surface that is virtually indistinguishable from the real thing. Hard to believe? Ask the hockey enthusiasts who skate there—teenagers who would normally complain about everything. They just love the artificial surface.

What's not to love? Because the artificial ice (known as Kwik-Rink) is cheaper to install and easier to maintain, the Trottiers can offer skate-time at half the cost that most rinks must charge. Monty Trottier confesses that when he decided to buy the product and install it, he and his brothers held their breath. "Hockey players are tough in more ways than one. We wondered if they'd like it." The response was overwhelmingly positive, even though there is slightly more drag on the skate. "This is actually a good training tool," says Trottier.

Skaters use their own skates. And skate normally. Even hockey stops are possible because a slight amount of the surface shaves off while braking, just like with real ice. The only difference is that it's not nearly as cold on the rink.

Although the technology has been around for almost twenty years, it has primarily been used in private homes. TNT Hockey now boasts the largest arena—96 by 85 feet—for this kind of skating in the Midwest.

The Trottier brothers will focus on training and three-on-three leagues. The upstairs offers shooting cages for practice (with the same surface) as well as a snack bar. "We might not sell quite as much hot cocoa," admits Monty.

Interested? Skate on over. Take Meridian north from downtown Indy. Go west at 169th, then left into Southpark. Or call (317) 896–2155. Be careful when you skate. It still hurts if you fall.

SOUTHEAST

SOUTHEAST

There's plenty to do in this part of Indiana, a region rich in history and easy to navigate. Lots of tour books cover it, and we've included a few of their favorites, like the world's second biggest clock and the Howard Steamboat Museum. But this book is about places you might miss, like the world's only cookie cutter museum, or the high school gymnasium that straddles the time zone, or the museum in Milan that celebrates one of the great sports stories of all time. You could spend an entire day in Fortville, where you can visit a calliope museum, a toy museum, and a church that's half soda fountain and half sanctuary. All in a square-mile area.

There's so much more. Like the guy who blows up hot water bottles. Yeah, he's in this section, too. Only in Indiana.

On Top of the World!
Bethel

It's the highest point in Indiana. My son said it was the lowest point of our vacation. But there it was, in Wayne County, just north of Bethel. We'd tell you more, but half the fun, actually ALL the fun, is finding it.

The map said we were 1,257 feet above sea level, but you can't see the ocean. You can't even see I–70. And you wouldn't even know from the drive you were going uphill. But, yes, this tiny off-the-road spot, just a few yards north of some hay rolls and fieldstones, is the loftiest place in Indiana.

Some people apparently get a high from this kind of stuff. There are even Highpointer Clubs, groups of folks who want to climb to the tippy-top of every state. It's easy to do this in Indiana, where the climb is officially listed at 20 feet. It's tougher in Alaska, which is rated a ten on the toughness scale and requires a 24,500-foot climb.

Indiana is ranked the sixth easiest high point to climb in America. It would probably be considered the easiest if it weren't so hard to find and you didn't have to jump a fence to get to it. We'd give you the directions, but listen to my son. It's not worth it.

Okay, okay. Here they are: From Bethel go north to State Road 227 for just over a mile to Randolph County Line Road (Bethel Road). Go west 1 mile and turn south on Elliot Road, then about a quarter mile to an access road. Park and hike back a few hundred feet. You should see a sign. I'm telling you again, it's not worth the trouble, except then you can say you did it.

No oxygen needed. I reached the summit of Indiana's highest point.

UNION PROBLEMS

*H*istorians seldom refer to it and the details are a bit murky, but Boggstown seceded from the Union in 1861. Here's what we do know. Shelby County had voted for Stephen Douglas instead of Honest Abe in the election of 1861. Turns out that Boggstown had more than a few Southern sympathizers, which led to a local resolution stating that if the nation were to divide, Boggstown would attach itself to the Confederacy.

Some called this a big PR move by the area's accomplished debaters, and it is believed that putting Boggstown on the map, not removing it from the Union, was the big motivation. For when Fort Sumter was fired upon and Lincoln called for a Union army, Shelby County residents responded, raising two full troops. Boggstown didn't offer a peep in protest, despite its resolution that is—believe it or not—still on the books.

Nowadays Boggstown is known more for its cabaret than its tie to the confederacy. For rip-roaring entertainment with songs you'll remember, call the Boggstown Inn and Cabaret on London Road (800–672–2656). If you don't remember all the songs, you'll not forget Queenie Thompson, who at age eighty-five plays the piano not just with her hands, but her feet as well. And then there's Vivian Cox, probably the only female rhythm and bones player in America. Take I–74 to the London exit and stay on London Road until you get to the Boggstown Inn. If you miss the inn, you have also missed Boggstown and a great show.

THEY'VE GOT GAME
Bridgeport

The largest gaming vessel in the world is in landlocked Indiana. Don't believe it? Look it up in the *Guinness Book of World Records*. It's called *Caesars Indiana* and it has all the grandeur that was Rome. With a few more slot machines. This mighty riverboat is four stories high, 100 feet wide, and 450 feet long. That's how big you have to be to hold 2,400 slot machines, 140 gaming tables, and seven themed casino areas.

Ready for an exciting ride down the Ohio River? Don't bet on it. While the ship is seaworthy, neighboring states don't cotton to gambling, so ships stay close to shore and within a dice toss of Bridgeport, in Harrison County. Nevertheless, the riverboat is certified and manned by a full crew including a ship's captain. They just don't go anywhere. Is that is a dream job or what?

There are actually ten riverboats in Indiana, but *Caesars* is the biggest. And most dramatic. Inside are magnificent Roman columns, gold-leaf molding, and the biggest chandelier in the world. One of the themed casinos depicts the burning of Rome. That's just to get you in the mood. For what, we don't know.

Take a chance on having a good time by calling (888) ROMAN-4-U. *Caesars* is geared to high rollers or low rollers. Bet a nickel at a time or throw in a $500 coin (two at a time, if you have the nerve). It's major Las Vegas. Name a game, you can play it. And they'd like you to play it, again and again.

Bridgeport is on the Ohio River in Harrison County 13 miles west of Louisville on Highway 111.

CHICKEN LIVER
Canaan

G ale Ferris is the ambassador of the United Nations of Chickens. It's something to crow about.

The sixty-four-year-old retired teacher and poultry farmer has been collecting exotic chickens since 1956. At one point, Ferris had breeds representing more than eighty different nationalities. "We had so many countries represented," he says, "we just started calling the farm the United Nations of Chickens."

The hobby began when Ferris took some of his eggs to market in Osgood, Indiana. When he returned to his farm just outside of Canaan, he brought with him a guest. From that first foreign fowl—a bearded buss-laced Polish—the United Nations was born.

Throughout the years, the Ferris farm has played host to blue-skinned Chinese silkies, Egyptian Fayoumis, bearded mottled houdans, and a black-and-white batch of bantams (white, buff, black, and barred). He has imported chickens from Japan, Germany, France, South America, and Indonesia. Yet even with all of the varied and exotic breeds Ferris has owned, he believes his first fowl is his favorite. "Bearded buss-laced Polishes are buff with white trim. They have a beard and gray scales on their feet," Ferris says. "I think they're stately and beautiful."

Ferris is happy to give free tours of his farm when he's available. (Donations are accepted and appreciated.) His tours won't be solely limited to chickens, though. Ferris is the founder of the Jefferson County Preservation Society. So guests will also learn about the area's historic buildings or the Pony Express mail route from Canaan to Madison—not a run for the

Like cluckwork, Ferris minds his chickens in the land of Canaan.
PHOTO: Ruth Chin

chickenhearted. He'll weave his two loves of history and chickens together when he can. "Some of the breeds have been in the country for more than one hundred years," says Ferris. "By keeping rare breeds, I think of myself as preserving history."

Canaan is 14 miles northeast of Madison, but you'd better call (812) 839–4770 before stopping by. Ferris is easily ruffled. By the way, Ferris actually has chickens that lay colored eggs. Easter was never easier.

QUAKER CHURCH
Cedar Grove

The Little Cedar Grove Baptist Church is the oldest church in Indiana still on its original site. It seems that back in 1811, the local congregation had been procrastinating about the construction of a new building for their service. So when an earthquake rattled through much of the Midwest that winter, many God-fearing people took it as a sign that it was time to build. Some accounts say the county was actually hit with a meteor shower, not an earthquake. Whatever the case, the parishioners opted for an all-brick church. Thank you, Three Little Piggies.

It hasn't been easy for the little church. The spring of 1913 brought torrential floods to the Indiana and Ohio Valleys, the greatest flood in Franklin County history. Water ate away at the land until the church hung—barely—over the eroded hillside. That was a big week for praying. But just in case, they fixed it, too.

Today the church is open year-round and is owned and maintained by the Franklin County Historical Society. Inside are the original pews, beams, and a replicated pulpit. The good-size stone-lined hole in the floor is where charcoal was burned to heat the building. Charcoal does not give off smoke—a good idea for when the nearby unfriendly Indians didn't need to know when the church was occupied. You can also see holes near the roofline for rifle muzzles.

There's no charge to get inside and the Franklin County Historical Society (765–647–5182) rents out the church for weddings and meetings. "We had lots of flower children marry here in the 1960s and '70s," says Martha Shea, former county historian. By the way, the doors of the church are never locked. "This prevents people from breaking in," she says. The church is located 2 miles south of Brookville on U.S. 52.

HERBAL THERAPY
Commiskey

If there were a prize for Indiana's Most Tranquil Setting, Stream Cliff Herb Farm would certainly be a top contender. The secluded farm, located near the tiny hamlet of Commiskey, has been attracting guests—both wanted and unwanted—for more than a hundred years.

Betty and Gerald Manning and their children, Elizabeth and Greg, are the fifth and sixth generations to tend the tidy gardens. These natural works of art are filled with thousands of plants, flowers, and herbs and fashioned like quilt patterns (dedicated to Betty's grandma, an exceptional quilter and gardener), as well as graced with ponds and fountains.

The Mannings welcome visitors to drop in for soups and sandwiches at the Twigs and Sprigs Tea Room, where the fare is seasoned with herbs and edible flowers from the surrounding gardens. They also attract budding artists by offering classes on cooking, gardening, and art. "It's our way of sharing our lifestyle," says Betty. "You want everyone to share the joy from gardening and art."

Well, almost everyone.

In 1836 the Mannings' ancestors received a platoon of unwelcome visitors. That was the year Morgan's Raiders, a division of Confederate soldiers, crossed the Ohio River and pillaged the farm. Although it's unknown whether they were drawn in by the pastoral gardens or by the scent of afternoon tea, the Raiders didn't stay long, and—incredibly—they left the farm intact. Maybe a delightful supper of finger sandwiches and herbal tea, combined with a soothing afternoon stroll through the fragrant gardens, persuaded them to continue their pillaging elsewhere.

The herb farm is located near Commiskey, 23 miles northwest of Madison, north of State Road 3 and State Road 250. For
more information, call the farm at (812) 346–5859 or visit the
Web site: www.streamclifffarm.com.

ON TRACK
Connersville

When Maurice Hensley retired from the U.S. Postal Service,
he did what most people do. He took up a hobby. Not only
has the seventy-five-year-old from Mooresville collected more
than a hundred railroad lanterns, he has driven his train more
than 500 times and never tires of operating it. "Railroadin' just
gets in your blood," says Hensley. "You feel like you're accom-
plishing something when you're handling a trainload of passengers." Passengers?

Hensley doesn't operate toy trains. He is one of thirty-five
engineers of the Whitewater Valley Railroad—the longest
steam railroad in Indiana. The train he typically operates is a
1948 "Alco," an American Locomotive engine that pulls vintage
open-window coaches and a woodside caboose. After eight days
of training and working a couple of years as a brakeman, he
finally got his chance to take the controls. After twelve years,
he has no plans to retire.

From May to October, Hensley drives to the WVR station in
Connersville so he can shuttle sightseers down to Metamora
and back, and he knows every rise and fall of those tracks. "I'm
kinda getting on to it," he says. Familiarity of the run has not
led to boredom, though. Hensley spots deer nearly every trip.
And he's always striving to make the perfect run, a nice
smooth trip absent of jerky stops.

Hensley's love for trains has led to a second career track. He doesn't get paid for operating the Whitewater Valley train, but the experience earned him a part-time job running a freight train from Connersville to New Castle. It looks like his training finally paid off.

The Whitewater Valley Railroad leaves Connersville at 12:01 P.M. on Saturdays, Sundays, and holidays from May to October, and a fare is charged. For more information, call (765) 825–2054 or visit www.whitewatervalleyrr.org. To get to Connersville take U.S. 52 from Indy, then State Road 44 from Rushville.

CRYING WOLF
Dillsboro

P aul Strasser never met a wild animal he didn't like or that he couldn't lodge. That's why his Red Wolf Sanctuary in Dearborn County is a haven for wild animals that need a home.

Strasser started his nonprofit organization in 1979 after purchasing twenty-three acres of land just outside of Dillsboro. Strasser, who has a degree in fish and wildlife management, was originally intent on saving the red wolf, an endangered species that ranged throughout Indiana, Kentucky, and Illinois.

But soon he expanded his mission to include all North American predators requiring some kind of medical or behavioral assistance and who are not ready to be released back into the wild. The twenty-one-acre facility now includes raptors, bears, bobcats, eagles, coyotes, owls, and buffalo. He has two remaining red wolves.

Most of the animals are rescued from people who have illegally harbored them or who have taken them in as pets and now can't handle them. In some cases they were seized by the state and given to Strasser because the animals can no longer fend for themselves in the wild.

Strasser, one employee, and several volunteers care for the animals, all enclosed in huge pens, maintained to be as close to natural habitat as possible. The predators are fed a steady diet of roadkill supplied by the state. "I've spent a fair amount of time butchering deer," says Strasser. Once animals are judged ready for return to the wild, they are released.

Education is a top priority for Strasser, and he conducts tours for interested tourists and provides programs for local schoolchildren (reservations required). Red Wolf is 3 miles west of Dillsboro on State Road 62. Call (812) 667–5303 or check out the Web site: www.redwolf.org.

POLICE POWER
Elizabeth

Craig Pumphrey of Elizabeth (Floyd County) is one police officer you don't want to tangle with. He's in the *Guinness Book of World Records* because he can take a frying pan in his bare (bear?) hands and roll it into a cylinder with a circumference of 9¼ inches.

His brother Paul wouldn't be caught dead doing something so silly. He's in the same record book for blowing up a hot water bottle in 59.3 seconds. Their cousin, Scott, can tear thirteen decks of playing cards in half in 30 seconds. He's in the *Guinness Book of World Records,* too.

Craig started doing feats of strength as a kid, but later when he and his friends got involved in music, he realized that muscle demonstrations might give their band some needed publicity. Now their band, Lucent, plays all over the country. Their

That's Craig Pumphrey's arm. There's more where that came from.
PHOTO: Zeromix LLC and Lucent; used by permission

grunge heavy-rock music is punctuated by demonstrations, which also include concrete breaking, bar bending, and phone-book tearing.

The Pumphreys are always on the lookout for new feats of strength. In fact, skillet rolling and card tearing were both new categories that Craig and his colleagues suggested to *Guinness*. *Guinness* liked them both and incorporated them into their book.

Many have tried to break the boys' records, but as of press time, they remain the champs. "I think this has really intrigued people," claims Craig, who travels the world defending his title, "because we're not all that big. We're just everyday common people."

Yeah, right.

You can reach these hunks and find out about their band by calling Ivan at (812) 248–0797 or via their Web site: www. lucentrocks.com.

TASTE OF RELIGION
Fortville

E nter the storefront on Fortville's main drag and you see the two signs: HEALING GRACE CHURCH and OLD-FASHIONED SODA FOUNTAIN. That's right. A great place to worship and to enjoy a fine chocolate soda.

That can't be. In the same store? A house of God and a house of Godiva.

Former pastor Mark Adcock admits that when he rented space several years ago for his new church, he toyed with the idea of dispensing with the soda fountain. Instead, he just decided to dispense: ice cream, soda pop, milkshakes, candy, and sandwiches. And the best chicken salad this author has ever had. Like you've died and gone to heaven.

The soda fountain had been there for nearly fifty years—at times part of a general store—so it seemed like an appropriate family touch for his growing congregation. Plus, long-time residents had a place in their hearts—and their stomachs—for the old place. So Adcock decided to combine the love of God with the love of ice cream.

Recently the Lord called Mark to new pursuits, so he and his soda fountain split to a new city. But the Lord worketh in strange ways. Mae and Joe Quintana from Indianapolis bought the place. Mae was running a yogurt shop in Indy and Joe was a minister with the Healing Grace Church. What a deal. Different denomination, new flavors, but the same basic concept.

The soda fountain—now called the Main Street Deli—is open every day but Sunday, of course. There's probably not another place like it in the country.

Take State Road 67 to Fortville and head on over to Main Street. Or call Mae at (317) 485–5050.

Sweet Jesus!

CHURCH LADY
Fortville

Phyllis Baskerville of Fortville spends most of her days and nights in a church. But she's not praying; she's playing. Playing with toys, in fact. That's thousands and thousands of toys that this seventy-five-year-old woman has amassed over the past five years. So many toys, in fact, that she purchased and moved into an abandoned Pentecostal church where she now lives and stores her collection.

The obsession with toy collecting began after her husband of thirty years took ill with Alzheimer's. The stress and frustration led her to a hobby that has created joy in her life and for all her visitors. Baskerville secures her playthings at antique shows, flea markets, and garage sales, but she is adamant that every toy be in perfect working order. "If it doesn't work, it doesn't go home with me," boasts Baskerville, whose first collectible was a doll named Jess.

After Jess has come a barrage of board games, lunch boxes, mechanical dolls, banks, thermoses, cookie tins, Disney memorabilia, promotional toys, posters, and children's books. They fill every nook and cranny of every room in the church. More than a few of her toys and dolls are truly priceless. And she knows which ones are. But Baskerville will not sell any of her toys. No exceptions. No way. Don't even ask. Yet she knows that she needs to find someone, someday, to take over her collection. "All this preserves the past," says Baskerville, "and I need someone who understands that to watch over my toys."

If you want to see them, check into the Ivy House (317–485–5339) right there in Fortville. Overnight guests get a special invitation to see Baskerville and her collection. Generally, her home is not open to the public, but give her a call and ask. Who knows? You'll love Baskerville. She's a doll.

TRUNK SPACE
Fortville

Elephants may never forget, but there are some elephants that can't be forgotten. Like the one on I–67 just outside of Fortville. The pink pachyderm was purchased almost thirty years ago by Paul Dyer, who first rented the goliath for $200 a month. Dyer saw the elephant as a good promotional tool for the front of his package liquor store. "Everybody loved the big guy," says Dyer, "so I bought him for $6,600. And it was worth every penny."

The elephant sits on a trailer so it can be moved when necessary or dragged in a parade. "Our biggest problem was people

Is that a pink elephant or have I been drinking? Both.

ramming into it," says Dyer. Apparently all the customers at the liquor store are not sober. Go figure.

The elephant is still there today, but he has had a few facelifts and paint jobs. His glasses were stolen once and the martini glass held by his trunk could use a new olive. The new owner, Don Hunt, wouldn't part with the elephant for the world. "That's part of who we are. When you start seeing a pink elephant, it's time to stop at Wagon Wheel Liquor."

If you're in Fortville ask about Paul Dyer's Calliope Museum, one of the few in the country. Dyer makes 'em, fixes 'em, and displays 'em. Lots going on in Fortville. It's worth a stop. Call Dyer first at (317) 485–5524.

No Loafers Permitted
Friendship

There are no loafers at Robin Dyer's business in Friendship. But there are lots of moccasins—maybe the best-made moccasins in the world.

The company was started in the 1920s by Dyer's late father-in-law, Walter Dyer, who learned the trade as an apprentice and later taught the craft to Carl, Robin's late husband. Walter Dyer's work was so well thought of that in 1933 he crafted a pair of moccasins worn by Charles Lindbergh on his historic flight.

In ninety years, the company's reputation for quality workmanship has never waned. Dyer's has made moccasins for Rupert Murdoch, Johnny Depp, and Billy Golden of the Oakridge Boys, as well as Lars Lindbergh, the aviator's great-grandson. Dyer's moccasins are revered by hunters and hikers, but they are also purchased by people who just like to wear them around the house, at the mall, or when they're in their jammies.

The cowhide for the moccasins comes from Switzerland and is then tanned in England. Swiss hides are superior because dairy herds are government protected from slaughter until they can no longer give milk. Dyer's also makes moccasins from native buffalo and lines the shoe with elk fur.

Robin Dyer begins the process by cutting the basic outline of the shoe, then her small staff of artisans craft the final product. Most shoes require three to five hours to complete and cost between $50 and $300, depending on which of eight styles you choose.

By the way, don't look for Dyer's Moccasins in shoe stores. You can buy them directly from Dyer's small showroom in Friendship or by mail order. And if you'd like to see Dyer's craftsmen—and women—making moccasins, call in advance (812–667–5442) and you might be lucky enough to see just how hard it is to make soft shoes. "Hours vary," warns Robin Dyer, "by when I'm in the mood and how much work we have to do."

Dyer's is located at 5961 State Road 62 in Friendship. Or put your tired feet up and see the moccasins from the comfort of your home via www.carldyers.com.

M *UZZLE* U *P*
F *riendship*

To the men and women of the world who love their muzzle loading rifles, it's a perfect friendship. That's because Friendship is the home of the National Muzzle Loading Rifle Association, a seventy-year-old organization that seeks to keep the history of muzzle loading rifles alive through research and competitions.

Muzzle loading rifles, which require a reload after each shot, were used from the founding of this country through the Civil War. According to John Miller, executive vice president, the group has over 21,000 members, many of whom find their way to Friendship twice a year for national contests in the spring and fall.

The pistols and rifles are authentic remakes of the originals (the originals would be much too costly), and the black powder used is identical to the original. While some contestants dress the part, shooting the part is what the competitions are really about. According to Miller, accomplished shooters who load and discharge from a standing position can rival today's modern shooter, who depends on scopes and eyepieces. Shooters stand between 25 and 500 yards away from paper targets as well as silhouettes of men and animals. There is no competition for speed of reloading, which would jeopardize the safety of the participants.

The competitions are twice yearly, the second Saturdays of June and September. For more information call (812) 667–5131 or take a look at www.nmlra.org. Friendship is on State Road 62, just east of State Road 129, southeast of Versailles.

PACK RAT
Greensburg

Some people collect mousetraps, some collect sugar packets, others collect business cards, but John Pratt of Greensburg collects collections.

He was hooked at age three on baseball cards, then addicted to beer . . . cans (in middle school). At age twenty-two, he fell in love with a Hogan's Heroes lunch box. Soon he had 150 lunch boxes. But he had no keychains, no flags, no *TV Guide* covers. It was downright embarrassing. So for the last twenty-five years, Pratt has collected everything. Which means he throws away nothing. The trash collectors love him.

Here's what Pratt collects: scripts, flags, fossils, artifacts, keychains, globes, beer cans, games, props, stubs, lunch boxes, newspapers, magazines, records, phone books, yearbooks, masks, books, *TV Guides,* dime novels, photos, comic books, basketballs, animation cels, index cards, View-Masters, old cameras, license plates, FBI wanted posters, big little books, rosaries, prayer cards, bibles, buckeyes, tin signs, coffee mugs, old scrapbooks, patriotic stuff, tennis racquets, pins, Burger Chef advertising, All-American Girls, Professional Baseball League memorabilia, movie banners, movie snack boxes, baseball

Collecting everything but dust. John Pratt has it all.

bats, postcards, float pens, matchbooks, Taylor Hotel items, TV books, Hoosier-author books, costume jewelry, sleds, bikes, plastic cups, bumper stickers, sports cards, Chinese fortunes, coloring books, programs, cardboard cutouts, old coins, buttons, collector plates, marbles, hats, seashells, videos, 8 and 16 mm films, coupons, toys, and baseballs. Whew!

Pratt moved back to his native Greensburg from Franklin in 1999. His massive collection needed a home so Pratt renovated a hundred-year-old barn. The last Monday of each month, he invites the public into the barn to wander through the displays.

You should stop by. If you can't make it on the last Monday, just call him at his bookstore (Pratt Books and Other Fun Stuff at 225 North Broadway) and he might give you a tour. Here's the number: (812) 662–7896. Don't call collect.

Say Cheese
Greenville

It's not easy to get Judy Schad's goat. It's even harder to get her goat cheese. That's because her product, made at her farm in Floyd County, is carried only by the finest groceries and gourmet shops in the country.

Schad was a doctoral student in Renaissance literature who realized in the 1980s that there was more profit in Camembert than Camus. Schad capitalized on a changing American palate and a growing preference for locally produced products. Working patiently (like aging cheese), she developed her technique to the point where she is now recognized as one of the finest cheese makers in the country.

Schad sells several categories of goat cheese (fresh, ripened, and aged), but all are farmstead, meaning that the entire product comes from her farm. To accomplish this, she and her husband play nanny to 350 goats that are milked electronically each day, the only part of the process that is not done by hand. "Everything that happens here is a circle. It begins and ends on the farm."

Under the name Capriole Goat Cheese, Schad ships almost a thousand pounds each week to gourmet grocery stores and restaurants from New York to San Francisco. Her goat cheese can sell for as much as $20 a pound. Kinda pricey, if you live in a Velveeta world. Want more info about cheese? Call (812) 923–9408.

SUGAR HABIT

Now this is sweet. Phil Miller of Greenfield is a sucrologist—a grown man who collects sugar packets. And he's not alone, although we couldn't find one other person in Indiana who does this. But Miller knows that the art of sugar-packet collecting is healthy in England and France, where annual meetings draw hundreds of people. Of course, they also eat calf's brains.

Miller stole (how else can you get one?) his first sugar packet some thirteen years ago in Ohio. Intrigued by a series of packets printed with images of the U.S. presidents, he was immediately on a sugar high. Now, 7,000 packets later, he won't claim he has the most packets in the world, just the most in Indiana. The person with the second most has about seventy-five.

Miller gets his packets from restaurants, friends, and from visitors to his Web site who want to feed his habit. Sugar packets are fun to collect, but they're not in the same ballpark as stamps and baseball cards. "There are no Honus Wagners in sugar packets," says Miller.

By the way, Miller is diabetic. I'm not making that up.

Want more info? Go to the sugar collector's Web site: members.iquest.net/~phillip. Miller doesn't want us to give out his number because he's afraid he'll be deluged with calls. Besides, if you want to start your own collection, you know what to do. Just don't get caught.

THE WRIGHT STUFF
Hagerstown

The birth home of aviator Wilbur Wright has had more ups and downs than he and his brother had takeoffs and landings. The aviation pioneer was born just outside of Millville in Henry County. The house suffered two fires, one in 1884 and another in the 1940s. In 1955 the state of Indiana tore it down after recurrent vandalism had taken its toll. Then in 1973 the house was reconstructed. Why? Who knows? Hey, this is the government.

The state still was not happy with tourist response to the historic site, blaming attendance on its very rural location. But that's where the guy was born. Some thought the place would fly if they moved the house up to Summit Lake, some 6 miles away. Locals were unhappy with this idea and convinced the state to give them three years to get the tourist attraction off the ground, and so the state of Indiana handed over the deed in 1995 to a group known affectionately as the "Birthplace Groupies."

Apparently, the state made the Wright decision. The Wilbur Wright Birth Home and Museum is finally taking off. Visitors can begin with the welcome center, then proceed to the birth home, a two-story house that has been reconstructed and furnished in a style reminiscent of America after the Civil War. Then it's on to the museum, where a replica of the Wright Flyer has been constructed, true to size and exact in all the details. Inside, a functioning wind tunnel shows the dynamics of flight. There are even plans to replicate the bicycle shop that the brothers ran in Ohio. Also on the drawing board is a timeline with sketches showing events that shaped the lives of the brothers.

The Wilbur Wright Museum had trouble getting off the ground.
PHOTO: Wilbur Wright Birthplace

Outside the museum is a jet fighter. No one really knows why. Probably a government idea again. By the way, some purists complain that the house is kind of a fraud because it is pretty much just a reconstruction. We don't think that's wrong. But it's not all Wright, either.

The museum, at 1525 North County Road 750 East, in Hagerstown, is open April through October from 10:00 A.M.–5:00 P.M., Monday through Saturday, and by appointment: (765) 332–2495.

SHOE BUSINESS

*H*is grave is in the shape of an anvil, testimony to a man named by the 1892 Chicago World's Fair as the World's Greatest Horseshoer. That's where William Jennings Wedekind displayed 350 horseshoes, 250 of which represented the newest and most improved methods of making horseshoes and shoeing the horse. His awards during the exposition were for workmanship, quantity of items displayed, the tools, and the tightness of his tongs. We don't know what the last one means, but no one was tighter. He also invented rubber horseshoes, which created a lot of talk among the horses.

Wedekind is also credited with developing improved swedges for racehorses. We don't know what that means either. But we do know that his technique was groundbreaking because the shoes helped balance the horse. There is nothing worse than an unbalanced horse.

Wedekind was offered $100,000 for his collection. He turned it down and now you can see the collection at both the Wayne County Historical Museum in Richmond and the Nettle Creek Valley Museum, at 96 East Main Street (765–489–4005), right in the heart of Hagerstown. While inside the latter, check out the incredible murals painted by Charles Newcomb at the turn of the century, which entirely surround the museum. Here, too, you'll see the first cruise control device, invented by Hagerstown's own Ralph Tettor in 1950. To visit Wedekind's anvil grave, ride over to the West Lawn Cemetery, just down the block. In fact, there are several offbeat gravestones in this tiny graveyard, including a rocket ship. Have fun!

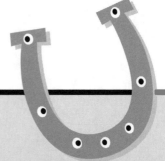

Here lies the world's greatest horseshoer.
And that might be the world's heaviest anvil.

SWEET TRUTH

*H*oosiers love their candy. We could do a whole book on great candy and ice cream stores. But we're not. I'm trying to keep my girlish figure. Here are a few of the traditional favorites. There are others. Lots of others.

Martinsville Candy Kitchen (90 North Main Street; 317–342–6390). Martinsville's Wonka was a man named Jimmy Zappapas who, in the 1920s, began making his famous hand-twisted candy canes. Today, the store makes twenty different flavors of canes, from peppermint to blueberry.

While the kitchen has switched owners, the sweet-tooth tradition carries on. In addition to candy canes, the new owners also make ninety different candies. For a different twist on Valentine's Day, they bend their canes into heart shapes.

Zaharako's Ice Cream and Confectionery (329 Washington Street, Columbus; 812–379–9329). Columbus's version of the Chocolate Factory is Zaharako's. It does not have Wonkavision, but the historic building does have two Mexican onyx soda fountains purchased from the St. Louis World Expo in 1905, a 1908 pipe organ, large glass candy cases, and plenty of oak and mahogany woodwork.

Along with a wide assortment of candies, Zaharako's also dishes out homemade ice cream, sodas, sundaes, sarsaparillas, and phosphates. The restaurant also cooks up some tasty cheeseburgers—made from melted cheese and chili sauce.

Schimpff's Confectionery (347 Spring Street, Jeffersonville; 812–283–8367). With Schimpff's being so close to the Ohio River, it is no surprise that the confectionery's most famous treat is fish candy. And I'm not telling a fish story, either. Maybe it was inspired by the fact that Schimpff's building has been flooded out by the Ohio on three occasions. Or maybe founder Gustav Schimpff simply thought it was a good way to lure more customers to his store.

Along with making its dandy candies, Schimpff's serves sodas, sundaes, shakes, sandwiches, and soups. The establishment also has the distinction of being designated one of Indiana's Hidden Treasures. Sightseers and confection consumers are always welcome.

DELIVERING HOPE
Hope

Albert Hitchcock was Indiana's first rural mail carrier and the man who invented the mail buggy on display in the Indiana Rural Letter Carriers Museum. The museum is in Hope because, in 1896, Indiana's first successful Rural Free Delivery began here—the second RFD in the country. And that accomplishment is celebrated in Hope's storefront mail museum. In addition to Hitchcock's buggy, such items as early mailboxes, old-fashioned sorting cases, and hot-water foot warmers are on display. "The carriers would use them to keep their feet warm while they drove their buggies," says Dale Davis, museum curator and retired rural carrier. "When the water got cold, they'd refill them with hot water at a farmer's house."

The museum is located on the town square in a small building where the public can visit, free of charge, any time they'd like. That's because the museum's entire collection can be viewed through the large display window, and it's illuminated twenty-four hours a day. They may as well proclaim, "See Indiana's only 24/7/365 museum!" With slogans like that, those tourists are signed, sealed, and delivered.

To find Hope—something we are all looking for—take I–74 south from Indy to State Road 9, then 9 south to Hope.

TIMING IS EVERYTHING
Jeffersonville

There is no excuse for being late in Jeffersonville. You can see the time day or night from more than 2½ miles away and the clock is accurate to within fifteen seconds a month. Okay, it's not the biggest clock in the world, but it's the second biggest. On the face of it, that's plenty big enough. Located atop the Colgate-Palmolive plant in Jeffersonville, this huge timepiece is 40 feet in diameter. The hour hand alone weighs 500 pounds and is 16 feet long. The minute hand is 600 pounds. A tiny motor, not much bigger than a sewing machine, drives the clock. At night, the clock is aglow with neon lights, so parents in Jeffersonville don't even bother to say "Do you know what time it is?" when the kids are late.

Jeffersonville is across the river from Louisville on State Road 62. If you can't find the Colgate clock, you are in the wrong city.

STEAMY MUSEUM
Jeffersonville

It may be the coolest museum in southern Indiana. And the hottest. The Howard Steamboat Museum in Jeffersonville is an eyeful before you even step inside. The stately Victorian architecture with its leaded glass windows is a wonderful introduction to the world of the 1890s, when it was built by Edmonds J. Howard, son of the world's great steamship magnate, James Howard, founder of Howard Ship Yards.

The twenty-two-room mansion cost nearly $100,000 to build in 1890 and is replete with original furnishings, intricate carvings, exquisite chandeliers, arches, and a grand staircase. Because master artisans at the turn of the century crafted the decor, visitors do feel they've stepped back into history.

While there are no full-size steamboats on the premises, models, photographs, paintings, and artifacts abound. Some thirty-eight steamboat models are displayed, including a large collection of hulls (known as half-breadths), particularly important because the Howards distinguished themselves in this aspect of shipbuilding.

If you do want to see a working steamboat from this era—there are only seven in existence—you need to cross the river and visit the *Belle of Louisville,* not a Howard steamer, but similar in style. Sadly, none of the 3,000 ships built by the Howard family remain in working order.

Tours take a full hour and have the personal touch. Interested? Then full steam ahead to 1101 East Market Street in Jeffersonville. For details call Yvonne Knight at (812) 283-3728.

Bonne Appetite
Knightstown

M ichael Bonne has a cookie cutter operation. No insult intended. None taken. According to Bonne, he is the largest producer of copper cookie cutters—and copper birdbaths—in the world. From angels to apples, baskets to bows, pumpkins to pigs, he seemingly has every large and small cookie cutter you could imagine.

Bonne's brimming Knightstown shop is a veritable warehouse of copper-colored creations. Along with his collection of cutters, he has stately birdbaths, weathervanes, napkin rings, jugs, whisk bowls, boilers, and shelves lined with many decorative items. There the master coppersmith expertly wields his old-fashioned implements and crafts his wares for the many tour groups, visitors, and customers that frequent his shop.

Bonne's nearby "factory" is a step into the past. One-hundred-and-fifty-year-old machines are used to bend and shape the copper wares. With hand-operated equipment, Bonne produces 10,000 cookie cutters per week. Once the summer rolls around, production kicks into high gear, and semis are used to haul away the cookie cutters to cookie makers all around the

The Cookie Cutter Museum in Knightstown. The shape of things to come.

country. There's a rumor he makes cookie cutters for Martha Stewart. Bonne isn't allowed to say, but he does look well fed.

Truth is, if you have a cookie cutter in your house with any fancy-shmancy name on it, Bonne probably made it.

And that's not all. Michael Bonne's Coppersmith Shop doubles as a museum, filled with antique tools and machines used in the 1830s. It's the world's only Cookie Cutter museum, with cookie cutters that go back hundreds of years, on loan from cookie-cutter collectors all over the world. I think we should have started the story with this, but sometimes it pays to read until the end.

Bonne's hometown of Knightstown is on the old National Road, U.S. 40, 35 miles east of Indy. Call for information at (765) 345–5521, or visit his Web site: www.MichaelBonne.com.

UNDERGOUND EDUCATION
Lancaster

E leutherian College's three-story structure, sitting atop what was once called College Hill, stands as a tribute to Indiana's pivotal role in the Underground Railroad. It seems the residents of Lancaster were not satisfied with simply providing a safe haven for escaped slaves. In 1848 Thomas Craven founded this college for free and fugitive slaves, deriving its name from the Greek word *eleutheros,* meaning freedom and liberty. They studied everything from the basics of reading and writing to advanced courses in Latin and Greek. And more than once students were whisked away and hidden in a nearby barn when slave catchers crossed the Ohio River and searched the campus.

Eleutherian was the second college west of the Allegheny Mountains to educate both Whites and Blacks together. Prior to the Civil War, fifty out of the school's 200 students were Black. After the war, when slaves were emancipated and other colleges opened their doors to Blacks, the college's enrollment began to decline. The college closed in 1887, and its buildings were later used to house a private high school. In 1938, however, the campus was completely abandoned. Today a museum and visitors' center has been built next to the stone structure.

Much of the building is in its original state. Visitors can read the school's rosters and seating assignments, penciled like graffiti on classroom walls. Century-old windows and chalkboards stand tribute to the college's builders, mostly volunteers and students working off their tuition. "The original bronze bell is still in the tower," says John Nyberg, museum director. "It's in a fragile state. The tower almost fell off the building four years ago."

Historic Eleutherian College is on 6927 West State Road 250, 12 miles west of Madison. Tours of the college and other

Underground Railroad sites in Lancaster, once the home of
Neil's Creek Anti-Slavery Society, can be arranged by calling
(812) 273–9434 or visit the Web site: www.eleutherian.org.

BACK IN THE SADDLE AGAIN
Madison

W hen Joe Schroeder closed up his family's little factory in
Madison in January 1972, he left behind a hundred-year-
old history in saddletree making. A saddletree is the inner
structure of a saddle, the internal wooden works supporting
the saddle that help the saddle sit on the horse, which in turn
helps you sit on the horse. There are saddletree makers today,
of course, but the hand methods used by two generations of the
Schroeder family are gone forever.

Well, almost gone. The folks at Historic Madison Incorporated were dedicated to restoring the one-of-a-kind Schroeder
factory, which sat suspended in time for twenty-five years. In
the spring of 2002, the Ben Schroeder Saddletree Factory
reopened as an industrial museum, a place where people can
walk into an operable, old-time woodworking shop and learn
how saddletrees were made in an era before cars replaced the
horse—a time when Schroeder saddletrees were being shipped
to all fifty states and around the world. Tours and demonstrations in the factory and exhibits in the family home will tell the
story of Ben Schroeder, his family, and his business.

Joe Schroeder left behind all of his family's equipment
(hand tools, belt-powered woodworking machines, steam
engines, a sawmill, a blacksmith shop, patterns) used to make
the wooden frames of saddles. Visitors also can discover other
Schroeder products like clothespins, gloves, stirrups, and even
lawn furniture.

They don't make saddletrees like they used to. But this is how they used to.

PHOTO: John M. Staicer, Historic Madison, Inc.

Visitors see exactly how the saddletree was made, but no instruction manuals were left. "We are reverse-engineering the process," says John Staicer, a local history buff. "We study the tool marks in the finished product and match them up with the machines and hand tools in the factory to figure out how the Schroeders made each of the five or so parts of the saddletree. Perhaps along the way we'll learn some of the family's secrets and preserve a craft tradition that helped settle our country."

To visit the Saddletree Factory Museum, take U.S. 421 to Milton Street, and head a half block west to number 106, in downtown Madison's National Register Historic District. For more information, call (812) 265–2967.

A QUA - D UCK
M e t a m o r a

It comes as no surprise that Indiana—the nation's leading exporter of duck feet and the Midwestern center for duckpin bowling—is cited in *Ripley's Believe It or Not* for something named, you guessed it, duck.

Metamora's Duck Creek Aqueduct is a one-of-a-kind covered bridge for canal boats. It's also the last of its kind. In the age when waterways were America's interstates, engineers employed their protractors to design and dig man-made water-ways across the country. When a canal crossed paths with a river, the designers sometimes went with the flow and used the river as part of their route. Other times, when crossing small streams, they designed overpasses, like the Duck Creek Aque-duct, that allowed canal boats to pass over the rivulets.

Speaking of being passed over, the aqueduct's life pretty much parallels Metamora's history. When the canal was built in 1846, the town seemed poised to be a burgeoning metropolis. But canal travel became passé and later, State Road 52 bypassed the town. Metamora slipped into obscurity and its economy went south for the winter.

Once the town recast itself from a trading center to a quaint hamlet of shops, it tapped into a steady stream of tourism rev-enue. The 60-foot aqueduct now shelters sightseers instead of merchants. Instead of aiding the transport of barges loaded with goods, it provides a photo-op for visitors aboard a canal boat, the *Ben Franklin II*.

Metamora is near State Road 229 and State Road 52, 11 miles north of Oldenburg and I–74. For more information, con-tact the Whitewater Canal State Historic Site at (765) 647–6512.

HOOP-DE-DO
Milan

Roselyn McKittrick wasn't at the game on March 20, 1954, the day that tiny Milan High School defeated monster Muncie Central for the state basketball championships. In fact, she wasn't even in Indiana; she was in Washington, D.C. with her husband-to-be. But that hasn't stopped McKittrick, who has

The Milan Museum. Old gym shorts on display. A brief look at basketball history.
PHOTO: Roselyn McKittrick

lived in Milan for almost fifty years, from being the number one cheerleader for this small-town team that played itself into history.

Ever since that game, McKittrick has been the premier collector of artifacts and memorabilia from that championship season. She even started a tiny museum right in the middle of her antiques store, Milan Station Antiques and Collectibles.

Although the area is small, fans from all over the country have visited her store, peering at original varsity jackets, a pair of trunks, video, posters, tapes, basketballs, newspaper clippings, and photos. Most impressive is the re-creation of the twelve team members' individual lockers, each chock-full of authentic memorabilia. Atop the lockers you can read the final score: Muncie 30–Milan 32.

As interest in that historic game grew, fueled in part by books and the Hollywood movie, *Hoosiers,* McKittrick found herself with more and more stuff and less and less space.

Enter the Milan 54 Museum Group, Inc., which purchased the old Ripley County Bank building, hired a designer, and plans to open a new museum dedicated to the arguably greatest of all Indiana sports stories. They're aiming for 2004, the 150th anniversary of the city of Milan and the fiftieth anniversary of what *Sports Illustrated* called the twelfth-greatest sports story of the century.

You can visit Roselyn McKittrick's antiques store now and in 2004 see the new museum by dribbling down to Milan via I–74 to the Milan exit, then through Milan, across the tracks, to 113 Carr Street.

BURNSIDE'S SIDEBURNS

*T**his is not a hair-raising story; it's a hair-lowering story.*
General Ambrose Burnside was not a particularly great
general. Word is, he wasn't a particularly great tailor either,
but he didn't stay long in that profession in the tiny town of
Liberty just prior to the Civil War.

When the Civil War broke out, Burnside accepted a com-
mand and found moderate success as a military leader, but
he seemed dogged by insecurities. When he was offered even
higher commands—once by President Lincoln himself—he
declined. Ultimately, he did take over the Army of the
Potomac.

We'll leave the particulars of his military successes for
historians to debate, but some of Burnside's mishaps are
legendary. He once approved a plan to place explosives 500
feet below a Confederate stronghold. The huge explosion that
followed effectively took out most of the Confederates. But
story has it that Burnside's men charged into the giant
crater and then couldn't get out, finding themselves at the
mercy of the remaining Southern troops.

But here's the important part. Major General
Ambrose Burnside let the sides of his hair (known
then as his "whiskers") grow down and over
the front of his ears. While he was certainly
not the first ever to do this, his celebrity
status resulted in what most etymolo-
gists agree was the beginning of the
term "sideburns," a simple reversal of
his two-syllable name. And that's why
we remember the general today. And
very few, except those in Liberty,
where there is a plaque on the court-
house lawn in his honor, even remem-
ber that.

By the way, this little piece is
called a sidebar. The general's hair
had nothing to with it.

L ETTER P ERFECT
Millhousen

J udy Checkley works at the post office in Millhousen, Indiana. Actually, she *is* the post office in Millhousen, Indiana.
For the past six years, she has been the only employee in what
is considered to be the smallest post office in the state.

How small is it? Maybe 4 feet by 6 feet—a mere hole in the
wall, or more accurately, just a corner of the Millhousen Grocery store. The building is at least a hundred years old and has
been a barn, an apartment, a liquor store, and who knows what
else. The Millhousen post office had been in the gas station, but
the station was sold in the late 1970s when the owner retired.
Vera Walters, who owned the grocery store across the street,
decided she wanted to be postmaster (she didn't like the sound
of postmistress), and lobbied Congressman Lee Hamilton for
the job. Vera held the job until 1995 when, at the age of
seventy-five, she decided it was time to step down.

There are no mail carriers in Millhousen. And there's no
sign proclaiming there's a post office. All of its nineteen customers pick up their mail in lock boxes at the post office.
Asked if her tiny post office accepts packages for overnight
delivery, Checkley replied, "We sure would; we just don't get
any." We're not going to tell you how to get to Millhousen, but
here's a hint: The zip code is 47261. And it takes three days to
get to Millhousen from Indianapolis. By mail, that is.

CASTING HER SPELL

Mercedes Russow spells trouble. She can also spell chrysanthemum. And because of Mercedes Russow, thousands of kids can spell just about any word they can say. And some words that they can't.

A tiny one-room schoolhouse in New Palestine was the home of Mrs. Russow's daily phonics course. Desperate parents, whose children failed in school to learn this basic approach to spelling, depended on her to cast her magic spell. And they'd drive several hours for this letter-perfect instruction.

Russow was first inspired by her mother, Pauline Troyer Banks, who began teaching school in Indianapolis almost seventy-five years ago. In the early 1960s, Banks developed a method for using phonics and was soon asked to teach the system to other instructors. As a teacher herself, Russow was intrigued with the program and assisted her mother in producing and marketing a phonics kit for teachers and homeschoolers. Banks continued to teach until she was ninety-four years old. Russow thinks that might be pushing the retirement age, and herself recently stopped teaching at age eighty-three.

Unlike with most spelling lessons, Russow says the kids swore by them instead of at them. "I've never had a bored kid," she says. "They come in the program mad and leave happy." And not just kids. A fair number of students are adults who never got the basics.

The same schoolhouse is still standing, but it is now used to assemble the phonics kits that Russow and her volunteers are selling within the state and will soon market throughout the country. By the way, Russow was a contestant in the Mrs. New York State Pageant in 1959. She might have won, but she admitted to reading Forbes Magazine and the judges were unhappy with her interest in money. Can you spell C-H-A-U-V-I-N-I-S-T?

INN BASKET
New Castle

Basketball is Big—REALLY BIG—in New Castle. From the basketball hall of fame to giant sneakers, New Castle likes its basketball super-sized.

When basketball superstar Steve Alford moved away from here, he left some big shoes to fill. One of them is in front of a hotel named in his honor. At the Steve Alford All-American Inn on I–70, there sits a high-top sneaker large enough to hold Coach Alford's entire starting lineup at Iowa University—14 feet high and 8 feet across. That's EEEEEEEEEEE, for you people into shoes. The shoe was actually donated by the Indiana Basketball Hall of Fame, where its mate can still be found. Inside the inn's lobby is a shrine to Alford. All of his jerseys from New Castle High School to the Dallas Mavericks are on display.

Alford was a shoe-in for the Indiana Basketball Hall of Fame, having starred at Indiana University and New Castle High School. For Indiana basketball fans, the Holy Land of Hoosier Hysteria is the Basketball Hall of Fame. All of the idols are honored there: John Wooden, Oscar Robertson, Bobby Plump, Larry Bird, and Damon Bailey.

At the Indiana Basketball Hall of Fame, visitors can sit in a locker room and hear one of John Wooten's pep talks or view video clips like Keith Smart's last-second shot that allowed IU to beat Syracuse and win the 1987 NCAA Championship. Once guests see how it's done, they can step onto a court, dribble away the final five seconds of a fantasy game, take the clutch shot, and experience the thrill of making their own winning basket.

No self-righteous Hoosier Hysterian could leave New Castle without visiting the New Castle Chrysler Fieldhouse—the world's largest high school gymnasium. The high school may have only about 900 students, but its fieldhouse officially holds 9,325. And on many Friday nights, crowds have exceeded 10,000 to watch such Hoosier legends as Alford and Kent Benson. Call (765) 593-6685 for more information.

New Castle is located 35 miles east of Indianapolis and 5 miles north of I–70 on State Road 3. The Hall of Fame is located on Trojan Lane, which is just east of State Road 3 on the south side of New Castle. Call 765-529-1891, or visit the Web site: www.hoopshall.com.

SAFE AND SOUND
New Palestine

H ere's a safe bet. Billy Jay Espich may be the only person in Indiana who collects and restores old safes. With a background in sign making and refurbishing race cars, Espich found the right combination when he sandblasted and repainted his first safe about twenty years ago. Now the Hancock County resident has an entire studio filled with safes and vaults, many rescued from old garages or landfills.

His safes usually are more than a hundred years old and weigh as much as two or three tons. "The old ones are out there," says Espich, "because it's really hard to throw one away." For him, the technique involves finding the old intricate designs that lie beneath the surface and creating a piece of art that looks the way it did a century before, when safes were not only functional but somewhat of a status symbol.

Typically, Espich buys an old safe for a couple hundred bucks, though often a person is just happy to get rid of the thing. Solid research is required to see what the vault looked like years earlier. Espich must be especially careful to preserve the original design and intent of the safe maker. "They don't

*Billy Jay Espich loves old safes. Functional and
beautiful. What a combination!*

make safes the way they used to," says Espich, who marvels at
the detailed designs frequently found inside the safes as well,
made for when they were displayed open during the day.

Some safes come to him locked. So how does he get into a
150-year-old safe without the combination? "I have someone
who is very good at that," smirks Espich, "and that's all I'll say."
Need a safe restored or cracked? Call him at (317) 861–6017.

TWO ROOMS, NO BATH

*T*hings are looking up at Micah Corsiatto's house in Richmond. In fact, if you don't look up, you can't even see the house. Corsiatto built a two-level, 110-square-foot tree house, one of the biggest you'll ever see. It's 25 feet off the ground. Real estate in Richmond is high, but this is ridiculous. Corsiatto made the local paper and several national papers; there was even a national TV story about the house.

Corsiatto never thought of himself as much of a carpenter, but he once built a sandbox. Why not go for the stars? Influenced by a scene in the movie Stand by Me and convinced he had the perfect tree in his backyard, Corsiatto set to work. Six weeks later, his tree palace with four real windows, two ladders, and a couple of bunk beds was finished. But it was too small, so Corsiatto, to the delight of his neighbors, put on a second story. His two kids loved it, too. "Another story, Daddy, PLEASE. One more story." You can see the treehouse from your car. Take Thirteenth Street in Richmond to 1305 Wernle Road and look up.

PLEASE HARP ON IT
Rising Sun

When folks find out that William Rees is a luthier, some people look up to him. Others just look it up. A luthier is any person who builds a stringed instrument. Ain't learnin' fun?

William and his wife, Pam, moved from Yosemite National Park in California to Rising Sun in 1999—possibly the first couple in American history to make that move. They have no regrets. Rees Harps remain the best-selling harps in the world.

Rees Harps are specially made for the harpist, unique in the industry. Artists choose the wood, ornamentation, and type of levers. A harp takes about two months, but plan on paying as much as $6,000 and that's without personal ornamentation. Not sure what you want? Enter Harps on Main, their quaint two-story building in Rising Sun, and spend time in the harp gallery, replete with harps, gifts, and Irish music. In two other rooms, tourists can see the harp-making process, including the crafting and stringing of the instrument by Rees's four artisans.

Rising Sun is on State Road 62, about as far east as you can go in Indiana and not be in Kentucky. Rees Instruments also makes psalteries. Look, I told you what a luthier is. You need to look this one up yourself. But you can call (812) 438–3032, or check out the 150-page Web site, TraditionalHarps.com.

SPEED DEMON

Rising Sun's J. W. Whitlock was an Indiana man quite proud of his Hoosier Boy. The doting father admired his boy's speed, good looks, and sleek design, and bragged about how easily his boy sped across the Ohio River. Whitlock brought Hoosier Boy into this world, but it was, of course, not his son. It was his world-class speedboat.

When Whitlock began tinkering with boats in 1907, top speeds hovered around 12 mph—bicycles could outrace them. Less than twenty years later, Whitlock christened crafts that pushed the envelope up to 60 mph and helped earn Rising Sun the moniker of "home of the fastest boats in the world."

In 1909 Hoosier Boy won every hydroplane race from Peoria to Buffalo. In the following years, Whitlock built a series of Hoosier Boys and continued his winning ways on America's rivers. His most famous race, however, took place on the familiar Ohio on October 9, 1924, when he made a record round-trip run from Cincinnati to Louisville. Dodging boat-sinking flotsam and rolling waves from a dozen barges, Whitlock clocked 267 miles in 267 minutes, 49 seconds, an average speed of just under 60 mph. While today's unlimited hydroplanes can go more than twice that speed, this record may never be broken, as the Markland Dam separates the two towns, preventing boats from making a high-speed, nonstop run.

Even though no one is allowed to drive Hoosier Boy, visitors are welcome to see the boat—and many of its trophies—at the Ohio County Historical Society Museum at 212 South Walnut Street in Rising Sun. For more information call (812) 438-4915.

2% SOLUTION

*H*ow old is 2% milk? Well, several weeks old in my fridge. But the concept of 2% milk goes back to 1948. And the man who invented what is now the best-selling type of milk in America still lives in Indiana.

Roy Roberston started work for the Salem Creamery in 1936. In the late 1940s, Aura Qualkinbush, one of the owners of the creamery—and a home economics teacher—complained about the chubbiness of some of her students. Robertson was asked by his boss to perfect a new product that had less butterfat. Skim milk had already been invented, but consumers had no choice between the 3.5% milk and the virtually tasteless skim, nicknamed "Blue John" by many country folks.

Robertson worked for more than a year tinkering with how to remove the fat and then replace it with other milk solids so that the taste would still please milk lovers. Robertson and his creamery never really got the credit, and Robertson never profited from his invention. Because he never got a patent for his discovery, other dairies were soon producing his 2% milk.

Robertson lives with his wife of seventy years in Salem, where the Stevens Museum (307 East Main Street; 812–883–6495) chronicles this little-known story.

By the way, 1% milk was invented by Robertson's half brother. Just kidding.

WHAT A DRAG
Scottsburg

Bob McAdams was looking for something to beef up his annual fall festival, known as CourtFest. He got more beef than he ever imagined. The idea was to get men to dress up as women, something that's pretty easy to do in New York City even without a contest, but is a little tougher in Scottsburg where such activity is frowned upon.

But there was little frowning at this event, whose purpose was to solicit funds for charity. Money was raised as well as a few eyebrows as local notables, including the mayor, donned dresses, heels, wigs, and assorted undergarments to become Scott County's ugliest "woman."

My son, the daughter. Fun times in Scottsburg.

PHOTO: courtesy of Bob McAdams

Fifteen men in drag paraded on stage, as the huge crowd showed their appreciation, hooting, applauding, and laughing. Then contestants answered provocative questions like: How do you handle unwanted advances? How do you stay in shape?

If you're interested in seeing the contest, it is held on the historic downtown square in Scottsburg the weekend after Labor Day. In recent years the annual Ugly Woman Contest attracted 10,000 people to the town, which is just off I–65, 82 miles south of Indy and 29 miles north of Louisville. If you're interested in being in the contest, call Bob McAdams at (812) 752–9211. He's not exactly picky.

Bubble Trouble
Seymour

When it comes to Beverly Randolph's clothing designs, one thing is clear, very clear: the clothing. Beverly makes clothing out of bubble wrap. Yeah, the clear stuff. The kind you use to protect your grandmother's vase every time you move.

Beverly's slogan: Put it on, pop it off.

The idea hit her while working at a local club. She noticed a woman whose bra had bunched up, creating an almost bubbly effect. "It was kind of like a Eureka!" says Randolph, who immediately knew that she could make a bra out of bubble wrap. "Then I realized I could get a little on the kinky side and have some fun with it."

Testing the market, she went on a nationally syndicated radio show in 1999 with a few models and soon the bra just took off, so to speak. Now Randolph makes panties, bras, skirts, boxer shorts, and wedding gowns—some thirty-eight products in all.

Bubblicious. Go ahead, burst my bubble.

PHOTO: Beverly M. Randolph

Randolph recognizes that many are going to want to burst other people's bubbles. "That's the point," she says. "The garments are fun and disposable." Prices range from $15 for hats, all the way to a thousand for a wedding gown. "I have a lot of great stories," says Randolph, not one of which we can print in this book.

And if this weren't enough, Randolph's products, called BubbleBodyWear, are actually manufactured in Seymour. Get it? SEE MORE. For info about bubble clothing, visit the Web site at www.bubblebodywear.com.

T R E E - M E N D O U S
Starlight

Let's just call it a would-be wooded area.

We're talking about an indoor forest—the only one in the United States. The Forest Discovery Center is filled with a variety of actual tree trunks and man-made trees and even has a flowing stream. The leaves are glued on one at a time and there's an ambient sound system that captures the sounds of the forest. There's a real forest down the street, but it's outdoors. Yuck.

A hike along the winding, wooded trail while listening to crickets, birds, and the gurgling stream sure gives the illusion of walking through an actual forest. And while computers obviously don't grow on trees, a handful of interactive screens are scattered about the path. While one informs of Indiana's native trees, another asks the question, "Are we running out of trees?"

The FDC's answer: "No."

The center, sponsored by Koetter Woodworking, believes in utilizing forests wisely and promotes the idea that forests are healthier if we all practice responsible management. To bolster that point, the FDC leads tours along its glass-enclosed skyway to the mill where guests see molding cut from trees and the resulting sawdust recycled and burned in the company's kilns, a testimony to its zero-waste policy.

Lewis hopes the hike through the indoor forest and the mill leave children better informed in forest management. "Some kids come here believing that trees have souls and that it's painful for them to be cut down," says Lewis. "We hope the kids leave with a better perspective." We sure hope so, too.

The center is located at 533 Louis Smith Road in Starlight and is open 9:00 A.M. to 5:00 P.M. Tuesday through Saturday and 1:00 to 5:00 P.M. on Sunday. For information call (812) 923–1590.

ODE TO A GEODE
Vallonia

P aul Wheeler doesn't have rocks for brains; he has brains for rocks. The eighty-year-old retired logger jokes that he has more than two million cerebral-textured stones, known as geodes, in the bins around his yard. Gazing upon the oodles of rocks, nearly ten to twelve truckloads of them, few would argue with his estimate.

Wheeler loves to talk about his rocks. In a single breath, and with the flair of Ross Perot, he'll tell you that he has . . . (inhale) "pink ones, yellow ones, orange ones, reddish ones, and white ones. I have some shaped like footballs and others shaped like bears. I have rocks resembling hoot owls and one that looks like a teddy bear with a bowtie. I have geodes as small as dimes and others as large as bathtubs. One geologist told me that I had one that was 100 million years old." Wheeler exhales.

People come from all over to buy his rocks, many of which were harvested from his creek. "I just got to picking them up and people started wanting 'em," explains Wheeler. Large geodes—the biggest top the scales at 275 pounds—are used for landscaping. Smaller, novelty geodes adorn many Hoosier desktops and mantels. Still others are carved into rings and other jewelry.

Some customers like whole geodes. Others like them split open, revealing the stones' mystical crystals. In all his collection, though, no two geodes are quite the same. "If you find two that are exactly alike," says Wheeler, "I'll give them to you."

Oh boy!

Paul Wheeler lives 15 miles southwest of Seymour, just south of U.S. 50 and State Road 135. Call before stopping by to see his collection: (812) 358–2573.

THE GRAPEST FESTIVAL EVER
Vevay

The good folks of Switzerland County have a lot to cheer about. And they stamp their feet, too. But first a little history: In the early years of our nation, this part of the country was a premier wine-producing area. But by the late 1800s, the wine production had, well, fizzled and today there is only one winery in the area. But who cares! Not the people of Switzerland County, who have deemed the week before Labor Day "The Swiss Wine Festival" to celebrate the Swiss who emigrated to America with the express purpose of developing a wine industry. When bad weather and plant disease ruined their crop in Kentucky, they moved to the Indiana Territory about 1802 and founded Switzerland County— the only Switzerland County in America.

A stomping good time in Vevay.

PHOTO: Switzerland County Welcome Center

The four-day-long celebration includes the obligatory music and food, but also features stine tossing. Stines are "rocks" of different sizes that are heaved by competitors in Olympic-shotput fashion. There is no record in Switzerland County of anyone ever training for this event.

The highlight of the festival is a four-day grape-stomping marathon. Competition is fierce, often pitting (this would be funnier if we were talking about olives) young against old, Democrats against Republicans, or rival corporations against each other. Those producing the most juice go on to defend their title the next year. Only top-seeded teams (now, *that's* funny) get prizes, but everyone can enter and share in the toe-to-toe competition. What happens to all that juice? Ann Mulligan, tourism director, admits that the liquid has to be tossed. "We can't find anyone who will drink it," she says.

The event is the week before Labor Day. Call the tourism folks at (800) 435–5688 for more information.

*B**IGGER* *THAN* *L**IFE*
Vevay

J osiah Leatherbury called himself an itinerant barroom muralist, not that it's a job there's a lot of call for. It all started when Indiana-born Leatherbury, estranged from his wife, decided to take his four horses and drift through Montana in search of . . . he didn't know what.

But one night in 1987, while Leatherbury was perched on a barstool in Roberts, Montana, the innkeeper asked if anyone could paint a scene on the back wall. Leatherbury, who could draw as a kid but had never painted a lick, volunteered. To his surprise, he was "pretty darn good."

Other bar owners heard about what he had done. Soon he was the West's only barroom muralist. Go figure. In 1989, when Leatherbury returned to his home in Vevay, in Switzerland County, he was commissioned by the county to paint a historic mural. Not just any mural, but a HUGE mural. "There

Mural, mural on the wall. Getting the big picture in Vevay.
PHOTO: Josiah Leatherbury

may be bigger ones," says Leartherbury of his 140-by-60-foot painting, "but I have never heard of one."

The mural depicts the county at the turn of the century, featuring horse-drawn wagons hauling hay down to the steamboats. Because Leatherbury grew up in the area and had heard old-timers talk so much about that era, he had a great feel for the image he wanted. His biggest problem was the necessity to step back—way back—to get some perspective on his work. After painting a minute or so on his electric lift, he'd have to get down and walk back an entire block to see his work. "And then people would want to talk to me, which kind of messed me up. I got real evil-tempered," admits the artist.

If you want to see the mural, just get yourself to Vevay, which is at the end of State Road 56. Trust me, you'll see it.

TALL STORY

Sandy Allen is a tall woman, the tallest in the world at just a hair above 7'7", according to the Guinness Book of World Records. In fact, she is taller than any NBA player in history. And her sense of humor is big, too. Ask her what she had for breakfast and she'll tell you "short people." This Shelby County native will also tell you that she was a normal-sized newborn, but by the time she was eleven, she was as tall as Michael Jordan. In fact, if an operation on her malfunctioning pituitary had not been performed when she was nineteen (she was already 7 feet tall), Allen might have rivaled Illinois native Robert Wadlow, who lived in Alton, Illinois, and is the tallest human on record at 8'11".

Unlike most giants, her life was not part of any fairy tale. She was essentially abandoned by her mother when she was just six and raised by her grandmother. And despite years of teasing and ridicule, Allen grew—girl, did she grow—into a warm, caring woman with a deep compassion for everyone.

Allen has traveled the world, been on dozens of network talk shows, and even made two movies. She wears a size 22 shoe, which necessitates specially made footwear. In fact, most of her wardrobe must be custom-tailored. The Indiana Pacers gave her a pair of Rik Smitts's size 22 shoes (Smitts was the Pacers' 7'4" center in the late 1990s); otherwise, finding sneakers would have been almost impossible and out of reach financially. Little else is out of reach.

Allen is pretty much confined to a wheelchair now. Her height and weight (450 pounds) make walking difficult. She also has a custom-made van, which she seldom uses, but she does remain on the lecture circuit. In order to appear on the Sally Jessy Raphael Show to promote her new book, Cast a Giant Shadow, Allen had to make the 600-mile trip by ambulance. But it was all worth it, because she had another chance to tell the world, "It's okay to be different."

The world's tallest woman and me. (That's me on the left.)

PHOTO: Courtesy John Kleinman

VERY SHARP BASEMENT
Waldron

D on Miller of Waldron is in this book because he has old tools in his basement. So how come you're not in this book, you might ask? You have old tools in your basement, too. Big difference—Miller's tools are as much as 50,000 years old. And he didn't borrow them from the guy next door.

Miller's basement is actually a museum filled with what might be one of the biggest private collections of Stone Age tools in the Midwest, certainly the biggest in Indiana. And most of the antique relics were found by Miller himself, a world traveler who, by his own admission, spends most of his vacations looking down, not up. The result is a prize grouping of arrowheads, spearheads, axes, malls (bludgeoning rocks), and fossils.

He also has an extensive collection of pottery, most of which was also literally uncovered by Miller and then carefully repaired. "It is rare," says Miller, "to find these pots whole, but all the pieces are usually nearby."

After visiting scores and scores of foreign countries, Miller can spin a story about virtually every one of the thousands of artifacts, recounting where he found it and what it represents in the evolution of tool making. His passion is contagious, especially when he places the tool in your hands, and you realize it was crafted by humans—well, sorta humans—tens of thousands of years ago.

And Miller has other stories, too. During one of his adventures in New Guinea, he and his party ran into a tribe of cannibals and were served for dinner. Let me rephrase that: They ran into some friendly cannibals and the cannibals cooked a hog and served them dinner. Yes, there are friendly cannibals.

He also has stories about meeting pygmies. Those stories are shorter.

Tooling around in Waldron. Don Miller
drives home a point.

Miller's museum is not open to the public, but here's his E-mail address: Wyman@svs.net. If you have a real interest in stuff like this, he would be happy to give you the caveman's tour. Drag your wife along.

Miller, by the way, has a Ph.D. in electrical engineering and worked on the first testing of the atomic bomb back in the early 1940s. We wanted you to know that in case you get tired of talking about tools.

INVASION OF THE WEIRD TREES

*T*he tulip tree has been honored as Indiana's official
tree. Sycamores have been heralded in the song, "On
the Banks of the Wabash." And now, thanks to the Division of Forestry, weird trees are finally getting the attention they so rightfully deserve.

And as it turns out, these mangled maples and
demented dogwoods are generating as much interest in
Indiana's forests as the stateliest sycamores ever did. "We
never received much media attention from our Arbor Day
promotions," says Sam Carman, Indiana Division of
Forestry's education director. "We wanted to come up with
a better way to pass on the importance of Indiana's trees."

Forestry officials sparked some interest when they
asked Hoosiers to submit pictures of the biggest trees.
Branching out to request the weirdest trees, however, has
proven to be a "tree-mendous" success. "We received 175
submissions from fifty counties for the booklet, Invasion
of the Weird Trees," says Carman. "I'm amazed in the
interest it has generated."

The booklet's B-movie copy adds to the already enter-
taining tree photos. One tree from Davies County looks to
be growing out of the asphalt. Its caption reads, "Chuck-
hole left unfilled in 1928 leaves highway department
headache." Another in Brown County has a large branch
that shoots back into the ground. "Genealogy tree probes
its own roots."

Carman's favorite entries are trees that have grown
together. Two trees—one of which resembles a camel's
head—in Vanderburgh County appear to be sharing a

"Mono Epidemic Linked to Kissing Trees!"

PHOTO: Tree in Northern Vanderburgh County—photo by Jerome Bockting

smooch ("Mono epidemic linked to kissing trees!"). A Bartholomew County tree looks to be spearing his neighbor's knothole ("Connected at birth, or a bizarre courtship ritual?").

The booklet proves that Mother Nature does have a sense of humor. Just ask a duckbilled platypus. Or the sickly sycamore in Owen County with the creepy face ("Tree surgeon sued over botched facelift!"). Wood you like to hear some more? I could go on for hours.

The latest version of Invasion of the Weird Trees *may be seen via the Indiana Division of Forestry's Web site, www.in.gov/dnr/forestry. Click on "publications" and scroll down.*

S PLIT D ECISION
West College Corner

The border between two states has to go through something. Maybe a forest, a field, even a parking lot. In rare cases, it may split a city. But a school gymnasium?

The town of West College Corner was platted by tavern keeper Gideon Howe in 1827. It lies on U.S. 27 in eastern Union County and is geographically split by the Indiana-Ohio state line. Today there are two distinct city governments, although these two tiny towns share some services. But in what has to be one of the most bizarre examples of multistate commerce, the trustees of West College Corner, Indiana, and College Corner, Ohio, decided more than fifty years ago to build a high school overlapping the border.

And it gets weirder. Not only was the high school split in half, but the school gymnasium is half in one state, half in the other. Which means that when you go down the basketball court, you are running from one state to another and, during daylight savings time, the time changes by an hour after every score because Indiana does not recognize daylight savings time. In recent years the high school was transformed into an elementary school, ending the traditional basketball rivalries, but the gymnasium remains a curiosity and attracts visitors from all over.

People in the area will tell you there used to be a tavern that was also split by the state line, creating a pub with two different drinking ages. We can't find any evidence of this, but it's a great story, no matter what state you're from.

Half in Ohio, half in Indiana. No penalty for traveling.

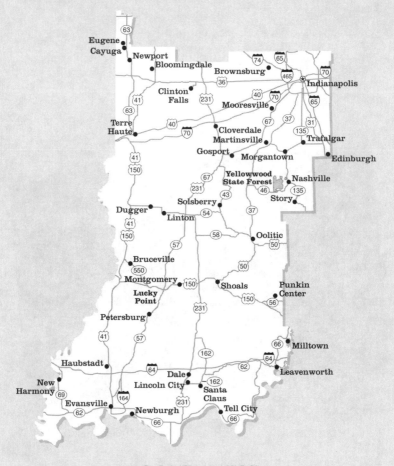

SOUTHWEST

SOUTHWEST

E veryone agrees that Southwest Indiana is the most beautiful part of the state, except the people who live in the
Northeast, Southeast, and Northwest parts. But there's no
argument that autumn is exceptionally breathtaking in the
Southwest, and here's where you can tour the boyhood home of
Lincoln and soak up some history. In this chapter we even
threw in some of that historic stuff, like New Harmony, just to
make you feel cultured. But we wouldn't want you to miss the
John Wayne Museum or the museum of mousetraps. Then
there's the tree with thousands of shoes hanging on the
branches and another tree with a quarter-ton boulder in it. You
can also visit a place where objects roll uphill. Or check out the
haunted library in Vincennes.

People in Southwest Indiana will still joke there's no way to
get to Indianapolis from the southwest corner of the state, but
that's okay because most of the folks that I talked to didn't care
much about visiting, anyway. After all, they have their own
share of neat stuff.

HOGWASH
Bloomingdale

R on Moore has never been a farmer, nor has he tended any livestock. He never owned a hog, and he never will. Yet that hasn't stopped him from amassing one of the Midwest's largest collections of hog oilers. Hog oilers are contraptions designed to apply medicated oil (hogwash, if you please) to a pig's skin to ward off lice and to prevent cholera. This probably is already more information than you need.

In the early 1900s, these swineskin soothers ranged in price from $4.50 to $12.00. Some manufacturers even promised a thirty-day, money-back guarantee. "But what respectable company would buy back an oiler that's been in the hog lot for a month?" jokes Moore. Names and designs were limited only to the inventors' imaginations. Moore has oilers by Watermelon, Hog Joy, Hog's Delight, Swine-Ezer, and Rub Hog or Die. He has some shaped like footballs, some painted like pool balls, and one that looks like a wheel of Swiss cheese.

Moore purchased his first oiler at a flea market seven years ago and has since pursued his passion whole hog. With more than eighty hog oilers ranging in worth from $50 to $1,500, he's the undisputed Hoosier Hog Oiler King. And though he ran out of display space years ago, he continues to root around for all the oilers he can find.

HOOKED ON TRAPS
Brownsburg

Tim Evans of Brownsburg is hooked on traps. Mousetraps, that is. The obsession began over thirty years ago when he and his father found an old mousetrap, circa 1915, while restoring an old home. "It looked more like a prison than a trap," says Evans, "and that got us interested. I mean, how many ways were there to kill a mouse?"

The mousetrap, a metaphor for the inventive spirit of America, has come in all shapes and sizes. So do mice, by the way. But more interestingly, the minds behind these traps, those steel-trap minds, have come up with dozens of ways to effectively dispense with our rodent friends.

After his dad passed away in 1993, Evans inherited over a thousand mousetraps (going back a hundred years) and the collection has continued to grow. Now his private museum is packed with contraptions whose makers were all in search of the better mousetrap. Evans cares little about the effectiveness of the trap, attracted instead to those traps that reflect a kind of Rube Goldberg approach to mice murder. He has traps that crush, electrocute, spank, decapitate, and strangle. One of his favorites has a mouse literally walk a plank into a little tub of water. The mouse is not blindfolded.

There's one trap where the mouse ends up in a kind of hamster wheel, then runs himself to death, unlike a hamster who knows when his little heart can't take it anymore and stops. "I don't know if that's true," laughs Evans, "but it's a great story."

Many of the traps were collected for their advertising and promotional themes. Even Bing Crosby had a mousetrap named after him. And Crosby's face is on the box. This drove Sinatra crazy. By the way, the bait of choice over the years, according

Catch this mousetrap collection: Tim Evans has
a thousand of them.

to Evans' research, is cheese or peanut butter. Don't ever say you didn't learn anything from this book.

Evans' museum is in his house. But if you love mousetraps and have absolutely nothing else to do one Saturday afternoon, you can reach him at JTEvans@netdirect.net. Hope you catch him at home. He deserves to be caught.

WAYNE'S WORLD
Brownsburg

J im Duncan only made one concession to his wife regarding his obsession with John Wayne: He agreed not to name his second-born son Rooster, after Wayne's character in *True Grit*. But other than that, Duncan has had pretty much free rein to pursue his love for the cowboy star. In fact, when his private collection of some four thousand items got too big for his house, he erected a small building in his backyard, creating what can only be called the John Wayne Museum. What else would you call it?

Jim Duncan loves the Duke. Name someone who doesn't. We dare you.

Although the 500-square-foot structure is too small for the 5,000 items displayed, Duncan is always expanding his collection, looking for unique items in catalogs, on the Internet, and at garage sales. He has been lucky, often finding old photos and statues at real bargains, but the enthusiast is not opposed to spending a few bucks, like on the $650 comic book featuring John Wayne. "The only thing I ever turned down was $5,000 for the shirt the Duke wore in *Donovan's Reef,* but I'll pretty much buy anything that's connected to the Duke."

Duncan has most of Wayne's movies on video, all the bios, magazines that sport the Duke's visage, Franklin Mint items, original posters, comic books, cutouts, and novelty items. Duncan loves to show his collection. Just be sure to call for an appointment at (317) 852–8437 or E-mail him at JimDuncan8@earthlink.net. And don't try to do a John Wayne imitation on the phone. Even Duncan is getting tired of that.

HIGH ROLLER
Bruceville

John Ivers loves roller coasters, but living in rural Indiana creates a problem. Every time he has a desire to take a thrilling ride, he has to travel a good 200 . . . feet. Ivers, you see, built a roller coaster in his backyard. Not some dinky Erector set contraption, but a coaster 188 feet long and 20 feet wide. It gets up to 25 miles per hour with a 360-degree corkscrew turn that still thrills the bejeebies out of the creator. He calls it Blue Flash.

Ivers, who had some background in mechanics, was still a little unsure whether he could match his plan with his vision. He worked without a blueprint, using parts he collected from around town or bought at the hardware store. He worked when he had free time and completed the project in just over a year.

If you build it, it will turn. John Ivers with Blue Flash.
PHOTO: Sharon Ivers

The coaster is a near work of art, attracting not only the neighbors, but newspapers and national TV shows as well. His kids and grandkids ride it; so do the neighbor kids. Is it safe? "Darn tootin' it's safe," says Ivers. "And I ride it first every day just to be sure."

Is it the only backyard, self-built coaster in the world? Probably not, say the experts, but it's probably the only one with a 360-degree corkscrew where the car travels upside down.

But John Ivers doesn't spin his wheels. The next project is on the drawing board—assuming he has a drawing board. How will it differ, other than being bigger, faster, and better? "I'll be able to take this apart and travel with it," says Ivers. You can call him at (812) 324–9030. Or stop by Bruceville. He's usually somewhere around . . . and around.

BRICK BUY BRICK

Karl Van Sant didn't have rocks in his head, but he did have bricks in his garage—a 900-square-foot garage with about 3,000 cubicles—and a brick in each compartment.

And not just any bricks, but designer bricks; bricks going back over a hundred years, each with the brickyard's name stamped into the surface. Nowadays brickmakers seldom take the time or trouble to personalize their products, so to collectors like Van Sant, the "autographed" brick was a great find. Van Sant started his hobby in 1975 when he and his brother, a bricklayer in Vermillion County, were working together and became intrigued by the way the different brickyards personalized their products.

Most bricks are red, weigh about 6 pounds, and look pretty much like the traditional products, but others are bigger and can weigh as much as 9 pounds. Van Sant, like a stamp or coin collector, preferred the perfect unused specimen, but most bricks come from previously standing buildings, so the collector must brush and clean his finds with acid and enhance the letters with white paint.

Van Sant seldom paid more than a buck a brick and often just traded. He collected bricks from almost every state and several foreign countries. He found his bricks at brickyards and landfills and attended meetings each year of the International Brick Collectors, where enthusiasts built on their collection, but they never built with their collection. "There is a guy in Texas with 8,000 bricks. I mean what the heck can you do with 8,000 bricks?" said Van Sant.

Karl Van Sant passed away in 2002. His wife, Mary, maintains the collection and will someday find a good home for the bricks, if you know what I mean.

WILD EXPERIENCE
Clinton Falls

For twenty-five years Larry Battson of Putnam County has roamed the halls of elementary schools throughout Indiana, herded kids into gymnasiums, and paraded wild animals in front of them. "I figure I've reached three million kids since 1978," says Battson, whose home in Clinton Falls is a preserve for more than sixty exotic species. Battson feeds and cleans up after lions, tigers, and bears (oh my!), as well as badgers, snakes, baboons, macaws, tarantulas, alligators, pythons, tigers, and coyotes, to mention just a few. Sorry to be such a game dropper.

Battson is unique in Indiana. Others will champion a certain type of animal, like raptors or snakes, and do a specialized show. But only Battson brings a virtual zoo to kids across the state and lets them get up close, sometimes closer than they ever thought, or hoped, they'd get.

Battson transports the animals in his van to each location—quite a job considering he visits more than 220 schools a year with only his wife, Cheryl, to assist him. Once in the school, Battson entertains the kids with a combination of snappy banter and important information about each animal, letting kids, when appropriate, interact with the creatures. "They laugh and learn," says Battson. "That makes it all worth it."

Food runs almost two grand a month and requires daily trips to the supermarket for huge quantities of meat, grain, and vegetables. "It's not a job," says Battson, who can never really take a vacation. "It is my life."

Larry Battson with two kids and a snake. Menagerie à trois!

Despite the fact that Battson does take wild animals into schools, no youngster has even been scratched. Not so for Battson, who claims the real danger is in feeding and transporting the animals. "I've been bitten by just about every animal you can name," he admits. He spent a week in the hospital at the hands (if it had hands) of a pesky rattlesnake.

If you want to book Larry Battson for your school, call (765) 739–6719.

B E L L M A N
C l o v e r d a l e

The late Francis Kennedy always heard ringing in his ears. And it certainly didn't take a doctor to figure out why. The source? More than 230 bells on display in his front yard.

It appears that Kennedy never met a bell he didn't like. For strewn about his farm, located just outside of Cloverdale, are church bells, school bells, steamboat bells, locomotive bells, and dinner bells. There are plain ones and elaborate ones. Some are cast from iron and others formed from bronze. On one chain alone, twenty-five bells dangle in the wind, ringing during strong gusts. Aside from the bells, there are windmills, bear traps, and a replica of Paul Bunyan's axe.

Locals know the place simply as the Bell Farm. (Apparently, the original name, Evergreen Farm, just didn't ring true any-more.) Two of the largest collectibles are next to the mailbox, anchored in concrete. "When the tires roll over a lever in front of the mailbox, the bells ring," says Kennedy's nephew, Paul Slaven. "My uncle did that so he'd know when the mail was here."

Kennedy died in 1988 and since then the paint has peeled off many of the bells and their wooden stands look badly weathered. Adding to the air of disrepair, the current mailman has taken a dislike to the ringing mail alarm. "The years have taken their toll on the place," says Slaven. We think he has used that joke before.

Cloverdale's House of Bells can be found just east of town, off State Road 42.

MUSIC TO OUR EARS
Dale

It's hard to leave Dr. Ted Waflart's place without feeling much better. And we're not even talking about his medical practice. We're talking about his museum: Dr. Ted's Musical Marvels.

While practicing medicine in the Appalachian Mountains, Waflart found a broken pump organ in an antiques store. Researching how to reconstruct it, he became intrigued with some of the older, mechanical musical instruments that he read about and started a collection in his home in the 1970s. He always dreamed of opening a museum, and his idea got a jump-start when he found a DeCap Belgian Dance Organ while traveling in Belgium. This incredible instrument is a veritable symphony with its accordions, saxophones, cymbals, and bass drum, to name a few. At 4,000 pounds with 535 pipes, it's an eyeful and an earful.

With the DeCap organ as its base, his collection expanded to include a turn-of-the-century Wurlitzer organ, calliopes, music boxes, player pianos, street organs, and dance organs—a total of sixteen mechanical musical instruments that play all by themselves. There's also a gift shop that sells moderately priced collectibles. Music boxes are the hot item.

His right-hand gal, Millie, runs the museum and give tours, whether to one person or a large group. "I once gave a tour to a double-decker bus, so I've decided that ninety-seven is my limit." Visit Dr. Ted's daily from Memorial Day to Labor Day, then weekends through September. They open up again for weekends in May. To find Dr. Ted's, take I-64 to exit 57, and go a half mile north. You can also call at (812) 937–4250 for information. But it's hard to hear on the phone.

DEAD CENTER

*R*esidents of Johnson County have taken the phrase "dead center of the road" a bit too literally. The proof can be found south of Franklin on County Road 400 South, a road intended to be a straight shot. In 1905, however, the builders were "encouraged" to alter their original plans. That's because Nancy Kerlin Barnett was buried where the road was platted and Daniel Doty, Nancy's grandson, protected the grave with a shotgun and suggested the road crew construct an alternate route. He threatened that anyone attempting to move her grave would join her.

The road crew presumably had heard of shotgun weddings, but this was probably the first time they thought of a shotgun bypass. But they heeded Doty's warning and split the road accordingly.

Over the years, cement markers stood as tribute to the standoff. Great-great-great-great grandson Don Hardin even recalls Boy Scouts tending the site by trimming weeds and planting flowers. "The cement marker was stolen twice by vandals," Hardin says. Since Nancy's relatives couldn't guard her grave with shotguns on a daily basis, they gently persuaded state officials to erect a sturdy, theft-proof historical marker. Officials heeded the family's suggestion and dedicated the marker in 1982. You can see the gravesite, approximately 5 miles south of Franklin's city limits on U.S. 31. Turn east on County Road 400 South and go about 1½ miles. But please don't bring a crowd. You know what they say: RIP.

MINERS ALLOWED
Dugger

Dugger's major celebration is a miner affair. That's because
Dugger's weeklong Coal Festival celebrates coal miners,
mining, and the company and the man for whom the town was
named. Francis Dugger, it seems, was a digger.

Dugger and Henry Neal platted the town in 1879 next to his
Dugger Coal Mine. His company was the town's main industry.
To honor the town's founding father, the residents changed the
city's name from Fairchild to Dugger.

One hundred years later, the coal industry is still a major
economic force. To mark its centennial, the town held its inaugural coal festival. According to festival organizer John
Booker, there's something going on every night of the week
during the late September gala. There's the firemen's fish fry,
the American Legion's free bean supper, and the Masons' steak
night. There are children's games, awards for the oldest and
youngest miner, softball, volleyball, soccer, live music, and a
parade.

The star of the parade, of course, is the honorable coal
miner's daughter. "Actually, now it's the coal miner's grand-
daughter," says Booker. "Most of the miners around here are
getting pretty old."

The really old miners are on display at the Coal Museum.
(Just kidding.) There is a museum, though, and it does have
many of the tools these miners used. There are mule harnesses
(used to pull wagons out of the mine), headlamps, coal jewelry,
and statues carved from the black fossil fuel. If you reside in
Sullivan County and don't know about this event, you're living
in a cave. You're certainly not working in one.

The Dugger Coal Festival is held in Dugger, 37 miles south-east of Terre Haute, east of U.S. 41 on State Road 54. For more information, call the museum at (812) 268–6253.

THAT'S ITALIAN
Edinburgh

It's a tiny chapel at Camp Attebury in Johnson County, no bigger than your average bedroom, but with walls replete with breathtaking Italian frescoes painted with the juice of berries, crushed flower petals, and even human blood to achieve the desired colors. It's quite a story. And one almost forgotten.

Camp Attebury played a vital role during World War II. Created in 1941 as a training camp for forces on their way to Europe, it later served as an interment camp for prisoners of war. By the middle of the war, more than 3,000 Italian POWs were being held in Attebury, awaiting their fate.

A strong religious fervor existed amongst the POWs, who asked the American chaplain that they be allowed to construct a small chapel within their recreational area. Permission granted, the captives—many of whom were skilled artisans—built this tiny church from raw materials they scrounged from the immediate area. Inside, the walls were hand-painted with elaborate religious designs, vibrant colors, and religious imagery. They dedicated it to the Blessed Mother and named it "Our Lady's Chapel in the Meadow."

After the war ended, Camp Attebury was deactivated, prisoners returned home, and the chapel fell into disrepair. Despite occasional halfhearted attempts at restoration, it seemed little more than a nuisance, destined to be destroyed when the first bulldozer was available.

In 1987 Ed and Betty Suding (Betty is legally blind), in search of a place to have a family reunion, came upon the chapel. When Betty felt the broken altar, she knew that something needed to be done. With some local grants and expert artistry, the chapel, on Route 52 between Franklin and Morgantown, was refurbished and lives again. The Italian Heritage Society of Indiana, in conjunction with the Indiana National Guard, presents an annual rosary mass and picnic at the site each year. Still, far too few know about the chapel. But now you do.

Visitors are welcome at the chapel. Call (812) 526–1112 for information, or just stop by. Take the Taylorsville exit (76) off of I–65, go three lights to Hospital Road, and follow the signs directly to the chapel.

TALKIN' TRASH
Eugene

Junky Joe's real name was Joe Gebhart, a man consumed by the love of junk—junk that he learned he could make money on. It all started in 1959 when Gebhart was rinsing off some old pieces of glassware that he had purchased for six bucks. When an antiques dealer offered him $18, Joe was hooked.

Before long, the garage was full of junk. I mean FULL of junk. And Mrs. Gebhart wasn't happy, especially when she couldn't park her '61 Valiant station wagon inside the garage during the dead of winter. And so, in the early 1960s, the extended Gebhart family erected several buildings to give the junk the home it so poorly deserved.

For over twenty-five years, Junky Joe collected every manner of trash imaginable. Another thing he collected every day was his grandson, Steve, whom he picked up at school and took junking. "We'd go all over," says Steve Axtell, who took over the business in 1980. "We'd clean out sheds, barns, black-smith shops—anywhere there was junk, we'd be there."

When Grandpa Gebhart died in 1986, Steve knew it was his destiny to stalk trash the rest of his life. Axtell now has seven barns filled with junk. That's seven buildings chock-full of every conceivable thing thrown out by man. And the stuff is scattered, with no rhyme or season to explain why some stuff is in one building and not another. "When I first bought the place I got things really organized," says Axtell, "but people didn't like it. That ruined all the fun. People like to dig, man."

What can you find at Junky Joe's? Let's put it another way. Junky Joe's has everything, the question is whether *you* can find *it*. Axtell claims that even in tiny Eugene, he gets visitors from all over the country. Recently several Parisians paid him a visit and brought an interpreter. "Just call me a junque dealer," smiles Axtell, a joke that is funny in print, but made no sense on the phone.

To find Junky Joe's from State Road 63, take State Road 234 west for about 1.4 miles until you see North Elm Tree, turn right at the corner and go half a mile. You can call first (765–492–3639), but Steve can never find the phone.

G H O S T   W R I T E R S
E v a n s v i l l e

T he Willard Library in Evansville, housed in a beautiful Victo-rian Gothic building, is the oldest public library in the state. Board members often boast about their original charge in 1885: "a library for use of the people of all classes, races and sexes."

Okay fine, but no one said ghosts were welcome.

Yet ever since 1937, when the library's janitor swore he saw the image of a veiled lady dressed in gray from head to toe, sightings of her apparition have persisted. Stories abound: unexplained running water, the inexplicable aroma of perfume, and smoky images caught by cameras throughout several rooms of the library. And the sightings continue to this day.

Whose apparition is it? Most believe (if they do believe) that it is the ghost of Louise Carpenter, daughter of the library's founder, who once sued the board of trustees because she believed her father had been unduly influenced to establish the library. When she lost the suit, she also lost all claims to the library's property. So after her death, Louise came back to haunt the building. Some say she will continue to do so until the property goes back to the living heirs of the Willard Carpenter family.

This may be the only ghost motivated by a bad real estate experience.

You can see some of these unexplained phenomena at a Web site dedicated to detailing all recent "confrontations" with the Lady in Gray. The Web site shows ghost-sleuthing photos of various rooms in the library. Look closely and you may see a hint of something from another world. Whether you think it's a glitch in the photo or a rip in the universe, is up to you. But the library's "ghost-cam" is worth checking out: www. courierpress.com/ghost. And so are the books in the library.

Happy haunting.

The Willard Library is at 21 First Avenue in Evansville. Phone: (812) 425–4309; www.willard.lib.in.us.

TRAVELING MAN

*E*vansville's John Clouse is a frequent flyer program's worst nightmare. He gobbles up miles like a Colts lineman punishes an all-you-can-eat buffet.

According to the Guinness Book of World Records, Clouse is the world's most-traveled man, having visited all of the world's 192 sovereign countries. He's even trod across places that are no longer on the map. What drives his wanderlust? "I don't like ballet," he says wryly. "So I have to have some hobby."

Apparently, wanderlust is hereditary. Another Clouse was at one time cited as the world's most traveled kid: John's son, George Chauncey Clouse. By the worldly age of five, George had voyaged to 105 countries. By the time he reached college, he'd added nearly 100 more.

John Clouse's love of travel inspired him to trek for months at a time when he was "going full blast." Now, however, with a handful of places he hasn't visited, he can be more selective. The two places at the top of his list are the Paracel Islands in the South China Sea and Bouvet Island, 1,800 miles southwest of South Africa.

While political restraints have caused him to postpone his trip to the Paracel Islands, Mother Nature has slowed his efforts to get to Bouvet. "The weather there is terrible," Clouse bellows. Then why go? In the spirit of adventurers everywhere, he adds, "Because it's there, of course."

We'd give you John Clouse's phone number, but he won't be home.

S PORTS R ACQUET
Gosport

John Baker is a singing evangelist, but that hasn't stopped him from being one of the top dealers of sports memorabilia in the country. While traveling from place to place to sing the Word in the 1980s, Baker often shopped at flea markets and antiques sales, feeding his passion for baseball cards and old ball gloves. Before long he was known on the circuit as the singing collector, a man who had both a great voice and a perfect pitch. Then it was on to trade shows and national conventions.

When Baker's hobby became a business, he moved it out of the corner of his son's room and into a 2,000-square-foot warehouse adjacent to his Gosport home. Inside he has more than a thousand old baseball gloves, each an endorsed model with names like Preacher Roe and Babe Ruth. "The Babe's," says Baker, "looks like a pot holder, no lacing, nothing, flat as a pancake." He also has leather football helmets, antique baseball bats, pitching machines, lockers, scoreboards, shoulder pads, javelins, vintage photos of high school sports, even Dick the Bruiser's shorts. "Not junk," cautions Baker, "but vintage stuff for collectors or theme restaurants."

People from all over the country come to shop at Baker's warehouse, but he's hit it big on eBay as well, where the memorabilia mogul spends hours each day buying and selling. His most expensive buy was a vintage Rose Bowl ring from the fifties, which he bought for big bucks and sold for bigger ones.

Baker's best buy? An eighty-year-old baseball glove with Ty Cobb's name on it.

"I paid a dollar for it at a flea market," he laughs. "Sometimes you strike out and sometimes you hit a home run."

There are a lot of ways to reach Baker: phone (812) 876–8580, or E-mail jjsportscards@hotmail.com, or drop by his Gosport warehouse Monday through Friday from 10:00 A.M. to 4:00 P.M.

John Baker wants you to lay a glove on him.
Preferably one with Ty Cobb's name on it.
PHOTO: John Baker Sports

TAKING THE PLUNGE
Gosport

R esidents of Gosport apparently took the phrase "take the plunge" literally. At least, when it came to holy matrimony. From the late 1800s to 1945, townsfolk would whisk away young couples after they exchanged nuptials and ceremoniously dunk them in a spring-fed trough. Over the years, historians have mislabeled the watering hole the "Chivalry Trough." The real word is "Shivaree," a mistake that's easy to make. But there's a big difference.

"Chivalry is how men should act toward women," admonishes Sue Trotman, Gosport History Museum curator. "Shivaree is an old tradition of treating newlyweds to a trick. It's a lot like a fraternity prank because it's their closest friends who dunk them."

The Shivaree Trough itself is not much of an attraction. The 8-by-4-foot concrete receptacle is hardly glamorous. It resides near the abandoned Brewer Flour Mill and is shrouded by weeds. Its legend, though, is certainly worth preserving. Trotman is unsure if the trough holds water anymore. She is sure, however, of the last couple who was plunged. "John and June Burns were the last ones to be shivareed in 1945," she recalls. "John was a great practical joker, so his friends were really looking forward to getting him."

The trough is located in Gosport, 21 miles northwest of Bloomington, east of State Road 231 on State Road 67. The Gosport History Museum (812–879–4873) can you get you there.

Why does a great wedding tradition like this fade while the "Chicken Dance" grows in popularity? We just ask 'em, we don't 'splain 'em.

CABIN FEEDER
Haubstadt

The Log Inn of Gibson County Haubstadt is the oldest restaurant in Indiana. Some of the logs in the structure date back to 1825; the remainder of the building is circa 1867. It also has breadsticks that old (just kidding).

Lincoln ate here in 1844 when, as a member of the Clay Party, he campaigned through the area and rested at what was then the Warrenton General Store and Tavern, a stagecoach stop for weary travelers. In 1965 the name was changed to the Log Inn.

The outside of the building has required some modern siding to protect the inner structure that goes back 175 years. Inside is virtually a log cabin, decorated with scores of antiques, many from the time around the Civil War. "Diners get a funny feeling eating here," says Kathy, the owner. This is not due to the food, by the way.

The restaurant seats 500 people, most of whom opt for the family-style approach. Best known for its fried chicken, German-fried potatoes, and cole slaw, the restaurant serves mostly locals because the closest real tourist area is New Harmony, almost 45 minutes away. But many hungry Hoosiers from the tri-state area make the Log Inn a busy place five nights a week (Tuesday through Saturday).

The Log Inn is a mile east of State Road 41 and a mile north of I–64. It does not have a Web site. But eat there and you'll be logging on in the old-fashioned way. Of course, you can call (812) 867–3216.

HAZZARDOUS DUTY

*T**he only** Dukes of Hazzard *prop more in demand than the original General Lee car are the cutoff jeans worn by Daisy Duke. Since there are only four known pairs of shorts—with one them in the Smithsonian—Travis Bell of Greenwood settled on the car that started it all.*

The flashy orange Dodge Charger, emblazoned with a rooftop rebel flag and "01" on the doors, flew over Roscoe's police car to open every show. Unfortunately that was the first and last jump the car ever made. "Anytime the car was in the air, it was destroyed," says Bell. And those who remember the show know that those cars were launched more than the space shuttle.

Bell estimates there are more than 300 General Lee replicas. As copresident of the Dukes of Hazzard *Fan Club, he should know. He owns one of the replicas and two of the squad cars. But his pride and joy—the mecca of all things holy in the Dukes of Hazzard—is branded with the ID plate of "Lee1."*

Bell found the car haphazardly during a Dukes paraphernalia gathering trip to Georgia. He met a man who was on the set when Lee1 made its fateful jump and who also knew of the junkyard where the car was abandoned. Some fifty cars were wrecked while the first five episodes were filmed. Most of them were smashed and sold as scrap metal. So when Bell laid eyes on Lee1, his heart raced faster than when he dreamed of Daisy.

It's in rough shape, with its trademark paint job veiled by a coat of green from when the car was patched up and reused in a later episode. "The rebel flag is still visible, barely burning through the paint," Bell says. But he has no plans to restore it. "I'd have to cut the whole thing apart and replace everything. Then it would be just another replica and not the original."

And that would truly be hazardous.

Travis Bell and General Lee. He'd still rather have Daisy's shorts.

PHOTO: General Lee Photo

TALL STORY
Leavenworth

One of the tallest mountains in the United States is in Indiana. You never knew this? Have you been living in a cave? That would have helped. The mountain is in a cave.

Indiana may be known for its flat, fertile farmland, but there are some rolling hills in the southern third of the state. And hidden within this crumpled, wooded landscape lies Indiana's Everest: Monument Mountain.

Monument Mountain is located 500 feet underground in Little Wyandotte Cave, near Leavenworth. Spelunkers do not need supplemental oxygen or a team of Sherpas to tackle this subterranean summit. Okay, so this mountain, made of fallen rocks and stalagmites, stands a mere 185 feet high. No strenuous walking or crawling is necessary to reach this mountain top, so don't expect to run into any Imax crews.

Nearby is the Pillar of Constitution—the world's largest stalagmite—35 feet tall and 75 feet around. Ashes, charred wood, and stone chipped from the pillar indicate ancient civilizations worshipped at the pillar or used it for a base camp before tackling Monument Mountain's summit.

True climbers may scoff at this underground mountain. We choose to write about it, however, because it is there. Wyandotte Caves can be found 43 miles west of Jeffersonville south of I–64. For information on tours, call (812) 738–2782.

Roaming Charges
Lincoln City

They call it the Buffalo Run Farm, Grill & Gifts—not exactly a name that national franchises are made from, but catchy nonetheless. And you can catch some great food here, especially if you're willing to try their famous ostrich and buffalo burgers. Of course, as you munch on this exotic fare, you can observe the buffalo and ostriches grazing in the field behind the restaurant, all watching and wondering if they will be your next meal.

The Buffalo Run Farm, Grill & Gifts. For more information about their gifts, please call their head buyer.
PHOTO: Gary Keener

Ice cream flavors reflect the ambience: Pioneer Pecan, Wild Frontier Strawberry, Choctaw Cookie Dough, Ostrich Orange Sherbet, and Chocolate Covered Wagon. There is also Mint Buffalo Chip. It's not what you think (we hope).

But the food is just half the fun. A visit to the gift shop is an absolute must for bison and ostrich fans looking for a buffalo-leg lamp, some poopaper (paper made from buffalo dung), ostrich feathers, or painted ostrich eggs. Frozen buffalo and ostrich meat are also available. You can even buy a buffalo-penis walking stick. I wish I were making this up.

The restaurant is just a mile from Lincoln's boyhood home, but as the eatery is only three years old, "Lincoln never ate here," says Kathleen Crews, the owner. "But he would have loved our ostrich burgers." Yes, but would he buy a walking stick?

You can drive your Lincoln, or Pinto if you're feeling lucky, to the Buffalo Run Farm, Grill & Gifts by taking I–64 to the Dale exit, then go south on Highway 231. Then left on Highway 162 for about 3 miles. Buffalo Run is open every day, but hours differ by season. Call (812) 937–2799 for more information.

MIDDLE AMERICA
Linton

Question: When can the center of everything be in the middle of nowhere?

Answer: When the U.S. Census Bureau decides that the center of the United States population is located in a rural Indiana county.

From 1930 to 1940, the center of the American people was near a reclaimed strip mine, off a dirt road, just outside of Lin-

ton, in Greene County. And they have the stone historical
marker to prove it.

Only God can comprehend the complicated computations,
logarithms, and elaborate geographical matrices the Census
Bureau used to pinpoint this spot. One thing we're certain of:
The formula could not be as complicated as the directions
needed to visit the marker.

Getting to Linton is relatively easy: Just take State Road 67
south, then State Road 54 west. Finding the road that leads to
the Linton Conservation Club, the park that hosts the marker,
is a bit trickier—especially since County Road 1100 is not well
marked. Once in the park, grab a compass and put on your
hiking boots. As the authors of *Indiana: A New Historical
Guide* describe it, the terrain is "geared more to the outdoorsman than to the sightseer."

A half mile of hiking over the wooded, undulating, sporadi-
cally marked trails of the reclaimed strip mine brings weary
tourists to the weathered marker. (That's if you've been lucky
enough to follow the map correctly.) After taking a couple of
snapshots of virtually nothing, all you have to do is find your
way back to your vehicle.

If you want an even more useless journey, visit Indiana's
highest point (but that's another story).

Lucky Charms
Lucky Point

For many years the area of White River flood plain was a
hotbed of UFO sightings. So many sightings, in fact, that in
the late 1980s the town marshal from nearby Monroe often came
down to Lucky Point to direct traffic. Needless to say, he was trying to control the extra tourists, not the extraterrestrials.

Lucky Point has a rich history of UFOs as well as grizzly ghost stories and unspeakable murders. The stories go back to the first white settlers in the 1760s, although even before then Native American oral histories reflected the belief that this area of the country was, well, different.

More recently, sightings have included black triangles in the grass, Big Foot sightings, quaking power pole lines, cattle mutilation, orange balls of light, and dead calves with their brains "surgically" removed.

A sheriff's deputy once reported seeing small slender beings with huge eyes peering from the windows of a spaceship. In another case, after a series of hundreds of nocturnal lights punctuated a pinkish orange glow over the area, the local weatherman checked his radar and saw nothing but squiggly lines. Apparently that means something.

By the way, Lucky Point got its name because hunters in the eighteenth century found game plentiful in this area of southern Knox County. The Point has also become a favorite spot for boys to take their dates for a little romance. Lucky can mean lots of things.

Take State Road 61 out of Vincennes to Monroe City. Lucky Point is just a couple of miles east of Monroe. Ask directions from Monroe, but most people will tell you there's not much to see. Of course, you could get lucky.

STAR POWER
Martinsville

The Goethe Link Observatory in Martinsville remains a secret even to nearby residents. Although it sits atop a mountain (okay, a steep hill), it is nestled behind a grove of trees and thus is nearly impossible to see from the road, a few miles below. That's probably the way Dr. Goethe Link wanted it.

The observatory was conceived and constructed by Dr. Link, a noted surgeon in the 1920s and '30s who made his name by performing scarless goiter surgeries. A renaissance man with a myriad of interests from hummingbirds to copperhead snakes, he had a fascination with ballooning but was discouraged by his wife, who felt that moonshiners, thinking he was a federal agent looking for illegal stills, would shoot him down.

That's the rumor, at least. One thing is sure: Link had a love of astronomy and was intrigued with the idea of a private donation to fund such a project. The telescope he commissioned and later donated to Indiana University was constructed entirely in Indianapolis and, at the time, was one of the eight largest in the United States. The observatory dome, which rotates like a fancy penthouse restaurant, weighs 34 tons and is 34 feet in diameter. The telescope, with a 36-inch mirror, weighs more than 5,000 pounds.

The observatory is now utilized by the Indiana Astronomical Society for its own members and to educate the public. More specific scientific research has been curtailed in past years because of increasing light pollution from nearby Indianapolis. But from mid-spring through mid-fall, the Society meets on the second and fourth Saturdays of each month and the observatory gate is opened by 6:00 P.M. Visitors are welcome to come, ask questions, and bring their own telescopes.

The observatory is at 1656 Observatory Road in Martinsville. Call first: (317) 831–8387, or E-mail motordrive@msn.com for more information. By the way, Mrs. Link still lives adjacent to the observatory. Her daffodil beds are legendary and delight Hoosiers every spring.

FAST BACKWARDS

They call him Mr. Backwards. And why not? Roger Riddell is the Ginger Rogers of stunt cycling. He can do what Evel Knievel can do, but he can do it backwards. But no high heels.

In 2001 Riddell drove his Harley Davidson 50 mph up a ramp and flew 62.5 feet backwards over five cars and another motorcycle. It broke his old record by 2 feet and it almost broke everything else in his body. It did get him in the Guinness Book of World Records. Riddell, who lives in Martinsville, has been doing this backwards thing for more than twenty-five years, and except for the fifty times he's broken one of his bones, he's loved every minute of it.

Riddell used to jump the normal way back in the 1970s, but Evel Knievel was such a big name at that time that Riddell knew he needed a little twist on his act to make it fly. The first time he jumped backwards was Mother's Day 1975. He did it in front of a crowd. He had never practiced it, never trained for it, and never really planned it. He just did it. "I still don't practice," says Riddle. "If I'm gonna miss, I'm gonna miss."

Despite all his injuries, Riddell has returned to jumping full-time, always looking forward to the next opportunity to better himself. "I want to stay in the Guinness book," he says. "Everyone wants to beat my record."

Not anyone I know, Roger.

Roger Riddell doing it the hard way. Not that there's any easy way.

PHOTO: courtesy of Roger Riddell

SHOE TREE
Milltown

I f you've ever wondered how that single shoe ends up on the side of the highway, you'll really be perplexed when you see the Shoe Tree in Milltown. For forty years folks have been coming from all over Indiana, Kentucky, and the rest of the Midwest just to toss a pair of old loafers, sneakers, or wing tips up in the tree.

There's some disagreement about how the tradition started, but Maxine Archibald, who for twenty years has owned and operated Maxine's Market just 6 miles from the tree, claims her father has the real story.

"He believes it was the Boy Scouts walking from Marengo Cave to Wyandotte Cave in the 1960s who often carried an extra pair of shoes. I guess they just started pitching them up in the tree," she explains. "And then the neighborhood boys followed suit. Next thing you knew, we had a Shoe Tree."

Now you know how to start your own.

The shoes are usually tied together and flung to the overhanging limbs of the mighty oak. "It's not easy to do," claims Maxine, "but the tree is sure loaded." No one has counted the shoes, but locals say it's easily several hundred pairs. Some of the shoes blow off in storms and find their way to the nearby creek, but for the most part, the shoe population is growing.

The Shoe Tree, which sits on Maxine's brother's property, has had its share of TV, radio, and newspaper coverage. We hate to say it, but there's no business like shoe business. Old State Road 64 goes right into Milltown. And you can't miss Maxine's place. Ask her where the tree is and she'll point you in the right direction.

GOBBLING UP THE COMPETITION
Montgomery

In Montgomery, turkeys aren't just for roasting. Apparently the farm-raised fowl are equally adept at racing—with a little help. At the annual Turkey Trot, hens are harnessed, leashed, and led down a hundred-foot track by child jockeys. Race times range from twenty seconds to two and a half minutes, says past chairman Scott Nally, who attributes the differences in speed to how well the jockeys control their tethered thoroughbreds. "Usually the turkeys are taller than the kids," Nally says. "Some will run straight down the track dragging the kids, and others take off and fly into the audience."

Some fowls are festooned with patriotic garb or decorated with driving apparel. Some children name their turkeys after Hoosier auto racers like Tony Stewart or two-time Brickyard 400 winner Jeff Gordon. Organizers, though, don't have the heart to tell the kids that there are no two-time trot winners. That's because the average life span of turkeys is fifteen to nineteen weeks, and the birds are raised to be dinners, not winners.

As if the spectacle of kids racing costumed turkeys isn't enough, organizers allow parents to cheer, videotape, and run alongside their children. Race officials, armed with turkey timers, also vie for space within the 15-foot-wide lanes to clock each participant. Multiply this by six to eight racing lanes and you've got a Southern Indiana comedy that could rival *Monty Python's Flying Circus.*

In Daviess County, the fun-filled family event is more popular than Thanksgiving. The townsfolk have more fun and the turkeys enjoy being the main event rather than the main course, for a while, anyway. The four-day event begins the Thursday after Labor Day. Turkey trotting, live music, mud volleyball, truck and tractor pulls, and pig wrestling draw nightly crowds of nearly 4,500—more than five times Montgomery's population.

Montgomery is 30 miles east of Vincennes on State Road 150/U.S. 50. For more information, contact Nally at (812) 486–3255.

R*ELIGIOUS* C*ONVICTIONS*
Mooresville

T he Assembly of God Church, at the corner of Harrison and Jefferson in Mooresville, is where John Dillinger baptized himself in a life of crime. On the night of September 6, 1924, Dillinger, age twenty, and Edgar Singleton were drunk on moonshine. The pair had wobbled their way through town and sat clumsily on the church's back steps. Unfortunately for grocer Frank Morgan, the church lay between his store and his home.

Dillinger and Singleton pummeled Morgan as he passed by and relieved him of his weekend's receipts ($150). Singleton escaped by car, Dillinger on foot. Not yet possessing the criminal prowess that made him a legend, Dillinger staggered back into town to inquire how Morgan was doing. Suspicious townsfolk alerted the police, who later arrested him.

A heavy-handed judge gave Dillinger the maximum sentence. It was during his incarceration, note many historians, that he honed the skills that would transform him from greenhorn thug into public enemy number one, from bumbling bandit to bank-robbing, prison-escaping legend. And they say prison can't rehabilitate.

Some Dillinger buffs like to go to Chicago's Biograph Theatre, where he was betrayed by the "Lady in Red," or visit the "escape-proof" jail from which he sprang himself. Still others

Before the Tommy Hilfiger look, there was the tommy gun look: John Dillinger dressed to kill. PHOTO: Lake County CVB—John Dillinger Museum

like to pay homage at the Dillinger Museum at the Lake
County Welcome Center. We suggest you go to the church.

"We can't all be saints." – John Herbert Dillinger

Heritage Christian Church is located in downtown Mooresville
on the corner of West Harrison and South Jefferson Streets.

UPHILL ALL THE WAY
Mooresville

Seeing apples roll up Kellar's Hill would have driven Isaac
Newton to discover hard cider instead of gravity. Gravity
Hill, also known as Magnetic Hill, can be found off State Road
42, just southwest of Mooresville. People have been perplexed
by this anomaly since the road was gravel and passengers rode
in rumble seats.

Here people park their cars at the bottom of the hill, put
them in neutral, and coast backward 50 to 100 feet. At the top
of the hill, they get out and try to push the cars back to the
bottom. To their (and our) amazement, the cars won't budge.
Curiosity-seekers also make the trek with buckets of water to
watch rivulets run uphill.

Folklore suggests an apparitional force from an Indian
witch doctor buried at the hill's base pushes the cars uphill. A
surveyor pooh-poohed such tall tales by proving the hill's
"crest" was actually 18 inches lower than its apparent "bottom." An Indiana University physics professor also helped dis-
pel the myth by noting that land contour, rock formations, and
the tilt of fences and utility poles add to the optical illusion.

The influx of traffic-stopping, bucket-toting tourists prompted
law officials to ask people not to stop in the middle of this now-
paved and busy byway. An article in *Outdoor Indiana* summed

it up best: "Heavy traffic coming at you may result in a differ-ent sort of gravity."

But if you want to try it, take State Road 42 for 1 mile southwest of Mooresville, turning right on Kellars Hill Road, which is usually unmarked (unless they marked it, but you'd better ask someone anyway because we hear they sometimes move the mark). Gravity Hill is 1 mile past this intersection.

MARRIAGE ON THE ROCKS
Morgantown

James "Smith" Knight had twenty children. Some say twenty-two. Some say twenty-six. But who's counting? Apparently no one. This was considered excessive even in 1894. But Knight built more than a big family; he built one of the most curious houses in Indiana.

The Rock House, as it is now called, was unusual for being constructed from cement blocks, a practice that would not be in general use for another twenty years. What makes the house truly unique is that before the concrete on each block set, Knight embedded stones, usually geodes, of varying sizes into the wet cement.

There's more. When he tired of stones in the cement, he starting throwing in personal items like coins, jewelry, dishes, bike chains, and pottery. Even a ceramic doll's head sticks out of the cement. Oh yeah, and a wild boar's jaw. Doug Strain, the current owner, is still discovering new things. "I walk around the house and see stuff sticking out that I never saw before."

The ten-room Victorian home has been a bed-and-breakfast for many years, a perfect place for parties, retreats, private dinners, and teas. Well, almost perfect. Doug Strain says that many believe the bed-and-breakfast is haunted by Isabel, Knight's first wife, who loved the house and is just keeping her eye on things. "She's a friendly ghost," says Strain. "At least that's what the clairvoyants tell me."

The Rock House is in Morgantown on 380 West Washington. Call for reservations: (888) 818–0001. If you don't think this is a neat place, you have rocks in your head.

PICTURE PERFECT
Nashville

S ometimes a picture is worth a thousand words. Sometimes it's worth about 500 dollars. That's true in Nashville, one of only three places in America where you can have a hologram (a true 3D image) made of yourself or a loved one. Or a pet. Or your mother-in-law.

Walk into Forth Dimension Holographics in Brown County and you'll know just how eerie (and realistic) this stuff is. You'll come face to face with Ronald Reagan, who you'll swear is right in the wall looking out at you. You'll see images of children, clowns, and pets, all in a three-dimensional presentation that is so lifelike it will give you the creeps. In some photos, the hologram is two channels, meaning that you can see different images that magically change with your viewing angle.

Sitting for a pulsed hologram is like sitting for a regular photo, but what the subject doesn't know is that the laser flash from the holographic camera is twenty billionths of a second. Needless to say, a slight movement won't make too much of a difference. Owner Rob Taylor can "develop" the film and have your photo in about five hours.

There's no danger involved, of course, unless your subject is the white Bengal tiger who took a playful bite out of Taylor's leg. His youngest subject was a nine-day-old baby.

Customers in his studio can buy stock images of animals, model cars, nature scenes, and limited edition fine art, but people with any real perspective on life opt for a personally commissioned hologram.

The studio is at 90 West Washington Street in Nashville, just off the main drag. You can call (812) 988–8212 or go to its Web site: www.forthdimension.net.

DEADLY MUSEUM
Newburgh

The Simpson Mortuary Museum in Newburgh isn't a hall of fame for morticians. It is, however, a place that preserves and displays the tools of the trade. Virgil Simpson, museum owner/curator, is a tough man to get in touch with. It's best to try to call him before noon on weekdays. That's because the retired mortician (his name still graces the family funeral home across the street) runs the museum more as a hobby and less as a business. "I'm not over there as much as I'd like," says Simpson. "I'm getting pretty old myself."

Once an appointment is made, Simpson gladly shows off his wares. Housed inside the centuries-old building are items once employed in his funeral home. Long before mobsters spoke of icing their enemies, morticians were chilling their clients with cooling boards. The bodies were placed atop the perforated top, while underneath, pans of ice kept the deceased cool during wakes. The boards proved especially useful during steamy summer days in this Ohio River town.

Other displays include gravity-fed and hand-pumped embalming apparatuses, wicker body baskets (used to pick up bodies in out-of-the way places like the woods), and some incredibly low mortician bills. "There's one bill that was only $25," notes Simpson. "Like everything else, that price has gone up."

One fee that hasn't been inflated, however, is the museum's admission price: free.

Newburgh is 10 miles east of Evansville. For tours, call the museum at (812) 853-5177.

PERFECT HARMONY—ALMOST
New Harmony

Indiana's southwesternmost county has the distinction of hosting not one, but two radical experiments in communal living. And both took place in the same location.

The first spiritual movement was in 1814 when George Rapp and his German band of Harmonists left Pennsylvania and founded the community of Harmony. Inspired by the belief that they were the chosen people and the end of the world was near, the Harmony Society toiled away on the banks of the Wabash, embracing a communal, celibate lifestyle.

For ten years, the industrious sect purchased nearly 20,000 acres (farming 1,450 of them), erected 180 log and brick structures, grew oranges year-round in greenhouses, produced and marketed fine silks and whiskey, and, in short, created a model settlement. But apparently too much of a good thing was, well, too much of a good thing. A decade of harmonious living, combined with the fact that the world didn't end, spurred Father Rapp to sell off his modern Eden to Robert Owen and move his flock back to Pennsylvania.

And the flock wasn't getting any bigger. Celibacy doesn't help that, you know.

Christening his village as "New Harmony," Owen went to work building a utopia of his own based on intellectualism and innovation. New Harmony's congregation of scientists, social reformers, artists, and writers are credited with many noteworthy firsts, such as America's first free public school system (offering equal education to boys and girls), a free library, a daycare center, a kindergarten, a civic drama club, and a trade school.

Today the atmosphere of nurturing both mind and spirit still prevails. Guided tours lead guests through the solemn hedgerows of the Cathedral Labyrinth, a maze where you could literally lose yourself for hours. Equally tranquil is the Roofless Church. The large, walled garden hosts a helmet-shaped structure that protects the sculpture "Our Lady of Joy" from the elements.

Those looking to tend the artisan within can join one of the annual gatherings of writers, artists, thespians, and philosophers. The New Harmony Inn promises to "offer visitors new horizons and sometimes healing experiences." Now that's a promise you'll never hear from Holiday Inn. Amen.

New Harmony is 26 miles west of Evansville on State Road 66. For more information call (800) 231–2168.

OVER THE HILL
Newport

It's been almost a hundred years since the first antique car grinded up the hill in Newport. Come to think of it, there were no antique cars in 1909, but the point is that this hill was a testing ground for automobiles of the early 1900s. Even

Henry Ford is said to have used the incline to test his cars.
Ditto, the Chevrolet brothers. By 1915 use of the hill had
declined due to financial problems and the fact that a new
decade of cars could easily navigate the 1,800 feet and 8½-
degree grade.

In 1968, interest in the hill was renewed by the local Lions
Club, which sought to reestablish the tradition in the Newport
Antique Auto Climb, a race that now attracts more than 80,000
folks every October. Race is the operative word here. This is no
beauty contest, but a demonstration of sheer speed by more
than 200 car owners who chug into town from all over the
country with their Model Ts, Model As, Reos, Packards, and
Studebakers. No car can be newer than 1942, and races are
divided into twenty-six classes.

They go up the same hill as in 1909. It's still 1,800 feet long.
The grade is still 8½ degrees. "Not only hasn't the hill changed
in ninety-five years," says Ed Conrad, one of the event organizers, "but neither has Newport. Not one bit, not an iota."

See or join the race the first Sunday in October. Call the
Newport Lions Club for more info at (765) 492–4220. If you're
driving an antique car, you can drive right into town after taking U.S. 36 about 60 miles west to State Road 63, then going 6
miles north to Newport. If you're driving a 2002 Honda, avoid
embarrassment by parking in Fountain County.

THE B-I-G PALOOKA
Oolitic

T he big joke about the Joe Palooka statue outside of City Hall
in Oolitic is that even he doesn't know what he's doing there.
That's selling the big guy short. You don't want to do that.

Here's the story: Limestone is a big thing in Indiana. (Did you know that NYC's Empire State Building is full of Indiana limestone?) There was even a move in the town of Bedford to build a limestone replica of the great pyramids of Egypt until Senator Proxmire came along and squashed the idea. But back to Joe. Joe Palooka, a comic-strip hero of the 1940s created by cartoonist Ham Fisher, was a boxer who ultimately enlisted in the United States Army. Fueled by American patriotism, the cartoon figure became a symbol of American might. Joe's nickname: "Defender of Justice."

In 1948 the limestone industry decided to build a statue of Joe Palooka to commemorate its hundredth anniversary. Two noted limestone carvers, George Hitchcock and Harry Easton, chipped away at the project at the Indiana Limestone Company and completed the work on the square in Bedford.

Joe got shuffled around for the next twenty-five years, and was often the victim of vandalism. In 1984 the Bedford Fraternal Order of Police donated the statue to Oolitic, where it now stands on Main Street between the town hall and the post office. People often arrange to rendezvous in front of the statue. You can't eat at Joe's, but you can meet at Joe's. And many do. Oolitic is thirty minutes south of Bloomington on State Road 37.

BUFFALO BURG
Petersburg

You've heard of buffalo wings and buffalo burgers. How about a buffalo burg? Petersburg is the only city in Indiana whose plat is based on a bison trail. According to "The Pike County History Bicentennial Edition," its streets "are laid out based on the Buffalo Trace, along the top of the ridge from Henry Miley's ash tree to Peter Brenton's cabin."

Maybe the town planners believed buffalo would return and did not want to hamper their migration. Or maybe they wanted their city to be mentioned in this book. Whatever the reason, the town built a main street wide enough to accommodate a stampeding herd of buffalo. So far, nothing.

Petersburg's expansive Main Street is 100 feet wide. And although no buffalo have raced down Main, horses certainly have. "My great-grandmother used to tell me about the horse races held every Saturday night," says Sandy McBeth, Pike County historian. "Everyone would come to town to do their trading, and then stay for the horse racing."

When the car replaced the horse, Main Street was wide enough for two lanes of traffic, a turn lane down the middle, and angled parking on both sides. "And back in the 1930s, cars also parked in the middle of the street," adds McBeth. This concept never caught on in Boston.

Main Street certainly suits motorcars, and it is ideal for parades. The people of Petersburg have parades to honor Little Leaguers, one at Christmas, and another during their Catfish Festival. But there isn't one that pays tribute to the honorable beast that influenced the town's design. Sounds like the bison got buffaloed.

Roam over to Petersburg, 33 miles southeast of Vincennes on State Road 61.

A L L   S O R T S   O F   S T U F F
Punkin Center

I n Orange County, in Punkin Center, on Tater Road, you'll find Add's Museum of All Sorts of Stuff, where, not surprisingly, you'll find a collection of, well, all sorts of stuff.

The museum is as muddled as that opening sentence. For Add's and the adjoining Punkin Center General Store are not really open for business anymore. Why write about a place that's closed? Because it's an interesting place, and it's not really closed, per se. Does that mean it's open to the public? Yes and no. Is there a tour guide? Sometimes there is, other times there's not.

Here's the scoop: Add Gray and his wife, Mabel, opened the store in 1922. Years later as the couple accumulated antiques, knick-knacks, and assorted relics, they decided to open a museum. In its heyday, a sample of the collection included saddles, swords, sleighs, scarecrows, chandeliers, and an old-fashioned soda fountain.

Add died some time back, leaving Mabel the sole curator and tour guide. If she's home, the museum's open. If she's not, you'll just have to come back some other time. "Nothing special goes on here," she says. "I don't do much. I've just been around here a long time."

Mabel's modesty is exceeded only by her longevity. She has trouble hearing, so it takes her some time to answer the phone or to get to the door. She does like the company, though. And she loves to reminisce and show off her wares. "Why don't you just come down sometime?" she asked me over the phone.

The next time my back-road wanderings lead me down Tater Road, I'll do just that.

Add's Museum can be found in Orange County, in Punkin Center, on Tater Road. Punkin Center is east of Paoli, just off State Road 56. Call Mrs. Gray before visiting, though: (812) 723–2432.

D *EAR* S *ANTA* C *LAUS*
Santa Claus

S anta Claus, Indiana, is a pretty popular place in the summer, what with its state-of-the art amusement park, considered by many the world's first "theme park." But it's wintertime when Santa Claus, Indiana, gets a little crazy. People just go postal.

The tiny town got its name in the 1850s when local residents discovered that the label they had picked for their fine city—Santa Fe—was already taken. The story goes that on Christmas Eve at the local church (also the town hall and school), when the townspeople were trying to decide on a new name for their hamlet, the church door inexplicably blew open and the children were said to hear sleigh bells. "It's Santa Claus," said one little girl. And there you have it.

Ever since then, Santa Claus, Indiana, has been the recipient of about ten thousand letters each year, letters simply addressed to Santa Claus. The U.S. Postal Service wasn't crazy about this, so it tried to change the name a few years back to Santaclaus, thinking that would stem the Christmas tide. Residents protested and got their name back. That's the spirit!

Believe it or not, each letter is answered personally by a contingency of "elves," local volunteers who want each child to feel special.

The original post office is now inside the Holiday World theme park but a new post office is adjacent to the park. Each year, right after Halloween, it's time to gear up for the onslaught of mail that has been pouring into this city for over a hundred years.

Other than the ten thousand letters to Santa Claus, the post office accepts boxes of pre-stamped cards and letters from people who want the Santa Claus postmark on their holiday correspondence. Last year, more than a half million letters got this special treatment.

Christmas and every other day in Santa Claus,
Indiana. It's crazy! Buy polar.

By the way, Santa Claus Land is now Holiday World &
Splashin' Safari. Apparently, Santa's name is hot in the winter,
but his appeal cools down in the summer. Go figure.

If you want to write Santa, send your letters to Santa Claus,
P.O. Box 799, Santa Claus, IN 47579. If you're more into riding
than writing, then visit the amusement park and hop inside
the world's largest enclosed water slide known as ZOOMbabwe.
It's 102 feet tall and 887 feet long and ranges in diameter from
9 to 12 feet. Wide enough for you know who.

Holiday World & Splashin' Safari is located at the junction of
Highways 162 and 245 in Santa Claus. From I–64, take exit 63
and drive south on Highway 162 for 7 miles until the road comes
to a T. Turn right and head up the hill; you'll see the parking lot
on the right. Call (800) 467–2682 for more information.

Scissors, Paper, Rox
Shoals

Since the 1800s, Jug Rock has been an Indiana roadside attraction—mainly because it is off to the side of a road, U.S. 50. Visitors have parked next to the heralded formation and memorialized it with illustrations, paintings, and photographs. Jug Rock even inspired state officials to dub its surroundings a nature preserve.

The 50-foot sandstone tower outside of Shoals is hailed as Indiana's most famous, most spectacular standing rock. Like most Hoosier rock formations, its appearance—an hourglass shape that must have reminded early pioneers of the earthenware jugs found in their log cabins—inspired its name. The formation is even topped with a sandstone cap resembling a stopper.

The city of Shoals has certainly done its part to honor the rock, and all of Shoals' athletes are known as Jug Rox. The school may have the only teams in America nicknamed after a rock formation. The *Pittsburgh Post-Gazette* thought so much of the moniker that the newspaper included the Jug Rox in its top-ten high school nickname list. The fifth-place honor placed Shoals behind Illinois's Hoopestan Area Cornjerkers, West Virginia's Poca Dots, Indiana's Frankfurt Hot Dogs, and Florida's Lakeland Dreadnaughts.

So when fans say these Shoals' teams rock, they mean it. Here are some additional fictional facts about Shoals:

School's fight song: Bob Seger's "Like a Rock"

Movie shown before each home game: *Rocky*

Concession stand favorite: Rocky road ice cream

Music played by marching band: Rock 'n' roll (preferably the Rolling Stones)

HARD TO FIND
Solsberry

Some call it the Greene County Viaduct; some call it the Tulip Bridge; others simply The Trestle. But most just stand there with their mouths wide open as they gaze upon it. It seems very out of place. Stand beneath the massive steel girders and you'll realize how insignificant you really are. Just what we all need.

The trestle is reported to be the second longest in the world (some say the third, but who's measuring?). Spanning 2,295 feet and 180 feet high, this steel and concrete structure is supported by eighteen towers. How could something this big be so hard to find?

When the viaduct was completed in December 1906, the Illinois Central tracks on that line extended from Indianapolis to Effingham, Illinois. During the days of steam locomotives, large wooden barrels of water sat on platforms along the viaduct for use in case of fire.

The history of the trestle is full of folklore and mystique. One story contends that more than a few bodies have been buried along the tracks, some of those deaths the result of some serious partying. Old-timers also remember dogs walking the trestle, then panicking when the train came rolling along, and jumping to their deaths.

The New York Central line operated on ground-level tracks until 1996 when the line was closed and the tracks were removed. The Indiana Railroad Company, which purchased the Illinois Central Line in 1985, uses the elevated tracks to haul coal from Greene County to Indianapolis.

You can stop at the general store in Solsberry and ask the clerk how to find the viaduct, except he won't call it a viaduct. Anyway, he'll scribble a map for you, but you can plan on asking about six people along the way. Then you'll end up following a guy in his pickup truck. And then when you see it, you'll wonder how you could miss it. IT'S HUGE.

Taped, Not Live
Story

T he story they tell at the Story Inn in Brown County is that a bunch of guys were downing a few cold ones and the subject of duct tape came up. And before you knew it, someone wondered whether you could do anything artistic with duct tape. So they called the 3M Company, makers of duct tape. As luck and duct tape would have it, 3M was looking for a promotion like this and voilà: The Celebrity Duct Tape Contest.

That's the story that Ole Olsen, director of the Southern Indiana Council on the Arts, tells people. And he's sticking to it.

The first annual contest—which will continue every year at the Story Inn—attracted more than sixty artists, with twenty making the finals. Each sculpture had to have a minimum of 75 percent duct tape on the outside, with an inner core of some soft material of choice, like newspapers or styrofoam. Celebrities sculpted included John Mellencamp, Sylvester Stallone, Charlie Chaplin, Jay Leno, and David Letterman. Olsen claims that both he and the artists, most of whom had never "sculpted" anything, were surprised at their own hidden talents.

Lucille Ball: revered on film, now honored in tape.

The first winner was a sculpture of Lucille Ball, her hair adorned with red duct tape, one of many designer colors available. The 3M Company asked me to mention that. For more information on this contest, call (812) 917–9811.

TWIST AND SHOUT
Tell City

Josephine Lahee has been doing the twist a thousand times a day, five days a week for the last thirteen years. That's enough to make Chubby Checker green with envy. But Lahee is not a professional dancer. She is a pretzel maker, one of two employees in charge of twisting—and baking—Tell City Pretzels. These tasty snacks have been a Southern Indiana tradition since 1858, the year master baker Casper Gloor, a member of the Swiss Colonization Society, landed at the Ohio River town and began to ply his trade.

Tell City Pretzels and snacks are sent all over the United States. "We've even shipped some off to England for somebody's birthday," says Lahee. It seems Europe's love for pretzels may have evolved from medieval times. Legend has it that pretzels were baked by monks who rewarded their pupils with them during prayer recitals.

Here in Indiana, the heavenly glazed and salted hard pretzels are still made from Gloor's original recipe. But don't bother asking Lahee about the secret formula. She'll never Tell.

Tell City is 52 miles east of Evansville on State Road 66. The company has brochures, but for a nice twist, visit in person. Call first at (812) 547–4631.

TERRE WATER
Terre Haute

I t's the largest living coral reef display in America and one of the country's largest saltwater fish and coral propagation facilities—and a mere 800 miles from the nearest ocean. Inland Aquatics in Terre Haute seems like a fish out of water, but it's worth the swim.

Inland Aquatics holds 40,000 gallons of salt water, hundreds of varieties of fish, and a total population that exceeds several million, if you count the really, really tiny critters. Many of the species occupy their own tanks to avoid infighting. They should try this at the Indiana Statehouse.

Inland Aquatics can sell you guppies for a dollar, a blue spot jawfish for $200, or a black tang for $400. Hey, how about a pair of blue striped clown fish for a thousand bucks? You can also find invertebrates, "live" rock and sand, hard and soft coral, and ornamental algae. Also, ecojars, cultured banggai cardinals, and deep oolitic sand beds. Not that you asked.

They can even offer you a tiny octopus. Tanks, but no tanks.

Most of the fish sold by Inland have been imported from warmer climes. While breeding tropical fish here would be nice, Mike Ames, manager of Inland, explains how that is virtually impossible because baby saltwater fish require live food, almost microscopic sustenance that cannot be successfully bred in large enough quantities.

Visitors to Inland can look at the fish storage area and filtration devices from observation decks. Except for an occasional guided tour, the public watches from the sidelines, although there is a retail area out front for people looking for an exotic addition to their aquarium.

To find Inland, drive your Stingray or Barracuda west on I–70 from Indianapolis and take U.S. 41 North. When you hit

the Courthouse, go around back and there's Inland. Way
inland. The retail area is open Tuesday through Saturday, noon
to 6:00 P.M.; Sunday noon to 7:00 P.M. Phone: (812) 232–9000;
Web site: www.inlandaquatics.com.

BARKING UP THE RIGHT TREE
Trafalgar

It's not easy to give up a thriving shiitake mushroom business. At least we don't think it's easy. But that's exactly what
Sherrie Yarling and Gordon Jones did ten years ago. After sup-
plying this gourmet fungus to Indianapolis's top restaurants
from their Brown County farm, they shifted a few gears and
are now—so far as we can tell— the only commercial producer
of shagbark hickory syrup in the United States.

It all started a decade ago when Gordon was tending to some
of the mushrooms that he cultivated from the felled branches
on his sixty-four-acre farm. A passing farmer offered to buy
some of the logs for firewood and noticed a few hickory trees
on the grounds. The farmer stripped off the outside of the
trunk and spun a story about how his great-great-grandmother
made a dynamite syrup using the bark of the tree.

The farmer was a little shaky on the details, but he ultimately did find the original recipe. Through some rather
sticky trial and errors, Sherrie and Gordon produced what
many believe is the best-tasting syrup you can buy. They were
about to embark (sorry, I had to use this somewhere) on a new
career.

Shagbark syrup goes back a long way. Research told Gordon
and Sherrie that American Indians—probably the Shawnee—
produced the syrup generations before the arrival of the pioneers.

The shagbark hickory is indigenous to the Ohio Valley, including Tennessee, Indiana, and Illinois.

And how's business? Well, it would be great if we could say "slow as molasses," but that wouldn't be true. Gordon and Sherrie work 24/7 producing their tasty product for the finest chefs in Indianapolis and have recently branched out to Chicago, New York, and California. When they sent a sample to Julia Child, she delighted them with a handwritten thank-you, which included how she enjoyed basting her ribs with the syrup. Other customers use it on desserts, waffles, corn cakes, Cornish game hen, and pork tenderloin. "There are a million ways to enjoy shagbark syrup," says Sherry, who encourages you to check out her Web site (www.Hickoryworks.com), where you can order syrup and download recipes.

R O C K I N' T R E E
Yellowwood State Forest

How did a quarter-ton rock end up in an oak tree, nearly 30 feet off the ground? Yellowwood State Forest officials don't know. But they certainly don't have any plans to remove the boulder anytime soon.

The refrigerator-sized boulder—christened Gobbler's Rock by an area turkey hunter—has resided in the tree's bough for as long as John Winne, Yellowwood's assistant property manager, can remember. And the anomaly has drawn as many visitors as it has sparked tall tales about how the boulder rose to such lofty heights. "The weirdest stories involve UFOs or black helicopters," says Winne. "My theory is that a logging operation used a skidder [a large bulldozer] and hauled the rock up there."

Another property manager believes that a local climbing club used a block and tackle to hoist the boulder into place. Once in position, the rock was used for rappelling. Another tale credits a tornado for ripping the rock from the ground and depositing it in the tree. "What we do know is that the tree did not grow under the rock and push it skyward," says Winne. "That's the only impossible theory. Anything else is entirely possible."

Yellowwood State Forest is just west of Nashville in Brown County. Hard to miss, unless you can't see the forest for the trees. Property managers can direct visitors to Gobbler's Rock, as well as to a smaller rock in another tree on the property. The best time to view them is in the spring, before the leaves block the view. Winne points out that it's safe to get as close as you'd like to the tree: "That oak is solid as a rock."

NORTHWEST

NORTHWEST

T he people in Northwest Indiana need to buy this book. And read this chapter. A man living a block from the Wizard of Oz Museum in Chesterton said he'd never heard of it. The local paper in Hammond didn't know they were doing exorcisms in a local church. Some people in Thornton had never heard of the Stone Chapel, a roadside sanctuary built from rocks. And it's right on the highway!

I met people in Crawfordsville who didn't know that America's only operating rotating jail was within a block. A policeman in Brookston didn't know where in this tiny city they made paper by hand.

I asked a local minister if he knew anything offbeat in Monticello and he said he didn't. Then his wife told me that he preaches his summer sermons in a drive-in theater. Not since the Ford Pinto have so many people prayed in their car.

There was one exception: Everyone in Knox knew where to find a front lawn decorated with rosary beads—made out of bowling balls.

Read this chapter and you'll be able to find it, too.

E L V I S   E X A M
A r g o s

Elvis has left the building—and he's moved to Argos to organize a festival to honor himself.

Okay, okay, Elvis does not live in Argos. But Elvis impersonator extraordinaire Quentin Flagg does. And at nineteen years old he organized the "Follow that Dream" Festival to honor the King of Rock 'n' Roll. At the inaugural event, Elvis impersonators of all ages shook, rattled, and rolled crooning the King's greatest hits. Flagg, who performs one to three shows every summer weekend, organized the festival to give his friends and family a taste of what he does on his frequent out-of-town trips. "Now my hometown can see what I do on weekends," Flagg says. They're so proud they can hardly talk about it.

Flagg began his Elvis career when he was fourteen. After seeing an impersonator perform at Merrillville's Star Plaza Theater, he felt the calling to be the King. He even told his mom that he would perform at the Star Plaza one day and in 2002, he did just that. He's performed at countless festivals, fairs, and concerts from the Bahamas to Memphis, from Las Vegas to Cleveland. He's also won several national Elvis impersonator contests and appeared on *Ricki Lake* and in an Elvis impersonator documentary, *Almost Elvis*. "He didn't hesitate turning down Jerry Springer, though," Flagg's mother, Maggie, says. "He respects Elvis's work and takes it seriously."

Flagg's parents are his managers and have watched him grow from a shy singer, scared of the flood of females seeking smooches, to a savvy performer sought out by booking agents. "I never thought I'd be a roadie for an Elvis impersonator," says his mom. "But it's been great." Good thing, because who other than mom knows how to make the best peanut butter and nanner sandwiches?

To book Flagg or hear an impersonation call (574) 892–5852.

M *UDDIED* W *ATERS*
A *ttica*

As a general rule, we're not big on visiting a place that isn't there anymore. But here's an exception: Kramer, Indiana, which is near Carbondale, which is near Attica. None of which are on most maps. When you get to Kramer, a tiny burg, you'll find a couple of burned-out buildings and a large smokestack. Exciting, huh?

Believe it or not, almost a hundred years ago, this was the site of one of the world's most famous health spas: Mudlavia. Let's go back to 1884 and Samuel Story, a man who suffered from severe rheumatism. Story discovered the curative powers of the local water and mud quite accidentally while cultivating his land. He drank the water while he trudged around in the mud for several weeks on his new farm, only to discover that the affliction in his legs had all but disappeared. Word spread and ultimately, H. L. Kramer, who was in the spring-water business, developed Mudlavia. The hotel he built became legend: marble and onyx partitions, German silver curtain rods, Tiffany windows. It was the grandest hotel of its day in Indiana—some say the finest east of the Mississippi.

Famous people like James Whitcomb Riley and John L. Sullivan were lured to Mudlavia more for the lithium-and-magnesium-rich water than for its five-star hotel. In fact, Kramer instituted a rather sophisticated advertising campaign

You can visit Mudlavia, but it's not there. So it's hard to find.

nationwide to spread the word of this magical water. The mud from the area was even packaged and sold. How much was hype, how much was true? Who knows?

In its time, Mudlavia was every bit as commercially success-ful as French Lick, maybe more so. Trains pulled in from all over the nation and were met by horse-drawn coaches to take guests to their palatial rooms. Once registered, guests were enrolled in complete health programs, involving diet, exercise, and emotional well-being.

So what's left? After several fires (and assorted hauntings) all that remains are a couple of charred buildings and an original smokestack. The spring still runs and, until recently, the water was bottled under the name Cameron Springs, then Perrier. The present owner, Dean Breymeyer, sells the water to bottlers who market it under different names. Breymeyer really believes the water is special, but you can't say that on the bottle.

To find Kramer, go to Williamsport, the largest city in War-ren County, and ask how to get to Attica, and then ask a state trooper who's been on the force for twenty years. He might know someone who knows how to get there. While on your trip, stop in Williamsport to visit Indiana's highest waterfall. It's a beauty and right in the center of town. Or you can try Dean Breymeyer's number (765–762–6559). He loves to talk about water.

WOLF PARK
Battle Ground

Wolf Park, in Battle Ground, has been the home of wolves, coyotes, foxes, and bison since 1972, ever since the concept of building a wildlife sanctuary where the public could do their own amateur research was founded by Dr. Erich Klinghammer. But Wolf Park is much more than a wildlife preserve. In many ways, it is the ultimate educational and research park in the Midwest, maybe the country, where you can watch these beauti-ful predators at work and play.

Although the wolves—more than a dozen of them—have been raised in captivity, they still exhibit all their natural behaviors and are a potential danger. In fact, Wolf Park may be the only known facility where wolves are permitted to "test" the herd. In twenty years, no wolf has taken down a one-ton bison, but the "audience" can witness the technique and posturing displayed by wolves when they are exposed to live game.

Another treat for visitors—and a treat for the wolves, as well—is the presentation of dozens of watermelons that are partially hollowed-out and filled with biscuits, pig ears, rawhides, and liver treats. Observing how the wolves eat the melons and yield to the other members of the pack is an interesting alternative to a day at the mall.

The serious student has several additional educational opportunities, including a five-day wolf behavior seminar that involves not just observation but collection of scientific data. Or you can adopt a wolf, pay for its upkeep, and receive regular updates on its life in the park. And on Wolf Howl Night, you can listen with other tourists to the intriguing and still somewhat mysterious chorus of wolves and coyotes as they "talk" the night away.

Take I–65 to State Road 43 (north); go north a mile to State Road 225; then turn right and proceed for 2.5 miles into the park. There are no picnic areas or campgrounds. This is the real thing. Times vary, so call (765) 567–2265 or go to www.wolfpark.org.

DAILY PAPER
Brookston

While in the tiny town of Brookston, we asked a police officer and a utility worker where Twinrocker was. Neither one knew. Kinda odd, because Twinrocker has been the premier manufacturer of handmade paper in America for the last thirty years. By the way, both guys knew where the German bakery was.

But the founders of Twinrocker, Kathryn and Howard Clark, care little about local notoriety. Their company proudly serves museums and state historical societies all over the country that need special papers to complete or restore historical documents. They have done work for the Lilly Library, the Brooklyn Museum, and the Library of Congress. "There's just no other place to get our product," says Kathryn, who started the business with her husband in San Francisco before coming east to work near the family farm.

Twinrocker also makes paper for watercolor artists with special needs, as well as for those with custom projects, including people who want the very finest wedding invitations. The paper comes in all shapes, sizes, and colors. And I think we need to mention this again: They make the paper by hand, an industry that had been virtually defunct in America for 150 years.

Tours are available and you can watch artisans make paper five days a week. You'll see each sheet formed one at a time as the mold is dipped into a vat of pulp. We won't tell you how the whole process works, but it's worth the trip to Brookston, 12 miles north of Lafayette on I-65. Take the first West Lafayette exit and head north on State Road 43 to town. Don't ask anyone in town where the place is—they won't know, but when you see the railroad on State Road 18, Twinrocker is right beside it. Be careful, it's easy to miss. Trust me. When you are lost, call (765) 563-3119 or (800) 757-TWIN. The Web site is twinrocker.com.

MADAME CHAIRLADY
Bunker Hill

Linda McCoy has been off her rocker for years. That's okay because thousands of others have been on it. Twenty-five years ago, McCoy and her family were in the furniture-refinishing business. To attract people to their store, just off of U.S. 31 near Peru, they built a huge wooden rocking chair, 13 feet high, and stuck it in their front yard where motorists would see it.

Rock the night away. And bring the family. There's room in this chair for everyone.

Today the McCoys are no longer in the furniture business, but the rocker still attracts people every day. "I can hear the screeching of breaks," says McCoy, who watches in delight as people "sneak" into her front yard to take a photo of a friend sitting in the chair. No need to sneak, of course; McCoy still gets a kick out of people's reaction to the mammoth chair. "Last year we had eight prom couples come out to snap pictures. It's been so much fun; we've replaced the chair twice."

You can see the chair right off U.S. 31 near Grissom Air Force Base. Bring a friend and a camera. And a huge cushion.

B LOWN AWAY
Chesterton

It seems that everyone at the Wizard of Oz Museum in Chesterton has had personal contact with a real munchkin. Even writing that sentence gives me the creeps, but it's true. Chesterton was the summer home of Frank Baum, author of *The Wizard of Oz* and about one hundred other books. Thus it serves as the perfect location of the annual Wizard of Oz Festival and the Wizard of Oz Fantasy Museum, which opened about twenty-two years ago (the festival came two years later in an attempt to revive the sluggish economy of Chesterton—and perk up sales in the gift shop).

The yearly festival attracts more than 100,000 people, including a handful of munchkins (excuse the expression) who make the journey to Porter County from who knows where. But munchkins are just a small part—a really small part—of the festivities. How about a Tin Man or Scarecrow look-alike contest, or a Wicked Witch cackling contest? There's Wizard of Oz food, whatever that means and, listen to this, a Dorothy-calling contest *(DAAARR-A-THEE...)*.

The Wizard of Oz Museum. You're not in Kansas anymore.
You're in Chesterton, Indiana.

When you're tired of all the activities, you can follow the yellow brick road to the gift store and sift through hundreds of collector items like mugs, cookie jars, magnets, charms, glasses, and salt and pepper shakers. The attached museum has a display of artifacts from the film. Most are re-creations but they're still fun to look at, like the mechanical Dorothy and an exhibit depicting the Emerald City.

Most of the stuff is pretty neat and fairly priced, but when I was there I bought a Wizard of Oz mug that I saw the next day for about two dollars less at Wal-Mart. If I only had a brain.

The museum is at 109 East Yellowbrick Road in Chesterton; phone (219) 926–7048. It is open Tuesday through Saturday, 10:00 A.M. to 5:00 P.M.; Sunday 11:00 A.M. to 4:00 P.M.; closed Mondays.

SHARP LADY

*O*h, *look! This is Dick's book. See Dick's book. Read Dick's book. Oh, if only Zerna Sharp were alive today. She could have written a blurb on this book's back cover.*

Miss Sharp was born in Clinton County and began teaching in Hillisburg and later taught in Kirlin. In 1924 she took a job with the Scott Foresman publishing company. While walking the beach one day, she observed young children at play. This, coupled with her teaching experience, created an image in her mind of how she wanted to teach reading.

Miss Sharp presented her ideas to educator William Gray, who asked her to develop the concept. Although she never wrote a story or drew a picture, her vision of the project was responsible for what is arguably the most successful series of children's readers in history. Miss Sharp oversaw each story line, each layout, and all the illustrations. She also conceived the idea of adding a new word on each page and then repeating the words to instill mastery of the vocabulary. I actually did the same thing in this chapter. You just didn't notice.

The Dick and Jane series came under criticism in the 1970s, the victim of changing times. See Zerna get angry. See Zerna curse.

Zerna Sharp died in 1981. Beautiful and intelligent, she never married. Her children, she once said, were truly Dick and Jane.

COURTING ARTISTS
Covington

If you're in good shape, the long walk up the Fountain County Courthouse steps in Covington will not take your breath away, but the murals painted on the walls inside certainly will.

The murals are the work of internationally known artist Eugene Savage, whose paintings can also be seen at Purdue University and the Indiana Statehouse. Savage, along with local artists, began painting them in 1937. Their mission: to depict the history of the United States. The murals begin on the bottom floor and work their way around the courthouse walls, providing a thematic and chronological trip through more than a dozen historical issues or time periods, including the tax issue, conservation, the arrival of the pioneers, the canal period, the Gay Nineties, the Civil War, and World War I. But the most thought-provoking aspect of the murals is their thematic depictions. Savage and his associates portray the just and the unjust; the wise and unwise; use of tax money; honest work; and avarice in government (portrayed by an octopus).

The project was financed by the Works Progress Administration during the New Deal era of the 1930s. When completed in 1940, the murals had an estimated value of $90,000. Today the estimate may be five times that, though many would judge them priceless. Over time, the murals had cracked and peeled and required major retouching by artists, and in 1982 a major renovation took place. While most of the murals had been painted directly on the walls, two canvas paintings by Savage needed special restoration, requiring experts from the Indianapolis Museum of Art.

The courthouse welcomes visitors and offers tours to school-children, who delight in this unique opportunity to learn history from a wall. To make your own appearance, head for Covington in Fountain County on I–74, then take U.S. 136 right into town. It's one court date you don't want to miss.

It's All Hurs
Crawfordsville

"It's called the Ben-Hur Museum, but it should really be called the Lew Wallace Museum," says director Joanne Sprague. "Problem is, no one would come." But they should. This tiny building in Crawfordsville was the private study of General Lew Wallace, author, inventor, diplomat, and soldier. Wallace was the author of *Ben-Hur,* the number one nineteenth-century blockbuster novel that outsold even *Uncle Tom's Cabin.* Wallace built the study so he could have "a pleasure-house for my soul, where no one could hear me make speeches to myself, and play the violin at midnight if I chose. A detached room away from the world and its worries. A place for my old age to rest in and grow reminiscent, fighting the battles of youth over again." Yes, that's the way he talked.

The museum, just one large room, is chock-full of artifacts that belonged to this talented Renaissance man. You'll see his paintings, musical instruments, and military garb, as well as the writing table where he wrote much of *Ben-Hur.* There's even a fishing rod with an enclosed reel that he invented. He was the original Popeil Fisherman.

Charleton Heston, the man who played Ben-Hur in the movies, visited this museum in 1993. He apparently asked for time alone with the general and spent almost an hour walking through the room. He loved the rifles.

But if you're looking for something spooky, take a look at the painting over the mantel, a portrait of the sultan of

The Ben-Hur Museum. Really the Lew Wallace
Museum, but don't let that get around.
PHOTO: Ben-Hur Museum

Turkey's daughter, which was given to Wallace in 1885. Notice
how the eyes of the young enchantress follow you around the
room—her shoulders even seem to tilt as you change position.

The museum is at the corner of Wallace and East Pike in
Crawfordsville, but it's a little hard to find and hours differ
from month to month, so call (765) 362–5769. Tell them you
want to visit the Lew Wallace Museum. It scores you extra
points.

CROOK MOBILE
Crawfordsville

L aw enforcement officials at Crawfordsville's old Rotating Jail were good at taking men and women with criminal records and turning them around. And around and around. To allow the authorities to better monitor their prisoners, rotating jails were built in the 1880s. The jail cells literally revolved on a turntable—not unlike a fancy penthouse restaurant—so that the sheriff or his deputies could have repeated face-to-face contact with each prisoner without moving from their desks.

As the two-story jail rotated, only one cell could open at a time, so jail breaks were virtually nonexistent. And the bad guys got a good deal as well, as every few minutes their cell would pass by the only window to the outside world. The jail was turned by hand, no easy job for the sheriff, who often had as many as thirty-two prisoners in custody. It is reported that many sheriffs made their wives do the turning.

Stories abound, like the one about Peg Leg, a local drunk and frequenter of the jail, who often stuck his wooden leg through the bars in the hopes of jamming up the gears. But Peg Leg broke his peg leg so many times that the deputies confiscated his artificial appendage whenever he checked in for an overnight stay.

The Crawfordsville rotating jail, the first in the nation and the last to still actually operate, accommodated prisoners until 1972, but it stopped rotating "guests" in the late thirties when there was concern that prisoners could not get out in time in a fire. Nowadays visitors can enter the jail and be rotated by museum caretakers. Apparently that's good for the gears, but it's hell on the staff.

This must-see in Montgomery County is located in Crawfordsville at 225 North Washington Street. Walk through the
museum. You may see some pictures of old relatives. Call on
your cell phone: (765) 362–5222.

LIKE WATER OVER A BRIDGE
Delphi

The people of Carroll County are proud of their bridges. Each
person has a favorite. And there are enough to go around.
And over. And under. For many the choice is Burnett's Arch. So
popular is the arch that the Carroll County Historical Society
adopted it as part of its logo.

In 1840 builders sought to carry the Wabash and Erie Canal
culvert over Burnett's Creek. Their solution was to construct a
stone arch over the creek, wide enough to carry the canal channel and the towing path. The canal, by the way, was a 438-mile
waterway that linked Lake Erie with the Ohio River. Locks,
aqueducts, and bridges permitted the canal to cross other bodies of water along the way. It was the longest canal in the West-
ern Hemisphere.

Burnett's Arch—an aqueduct, really—is an architectural phenomenon, not just because it's still around after 160 years, but
also because the bridge was built without mortar. This was
accomplished by using walnut timbers and stone slabs from a
nearby quarry, all cut to fit. So strong was the structure that it
supported the weight of the canal, the boats, and the towpath
with horses, people, and supplies. The limestone slabs are as
large as 12 feet in length and 2 feet thick.

Burnett's Arch is the only remaining bridge of its kind, and
it may be the oldest operating bridge in Indiana. When the

Wabash and Erie Canal closed in 1874, the arch sat dormant
for a while before continuing as a roadway bridge, a testimony
to the incredible engineering accomplishment of the day. Today
a similar structure would probably require engineers with computers and high-tech equipment. But according to Bob Conner
of the Carroll County Historical Society, "Those guys did it
with a compass and a pencil."

Total access to the arch is limited due to safety reasons, and
the best viewing area is on private property. But there is a
movement afoot to get the arch on the National Historic Register and purchase the adjacent land. From the Delphi Courthouse, turn north on Wilson Street. Cross the Wabash River,
turn east, and follow the Towpath Road through Lockport. Burnett's Creek Arch is a quarter mile east. But it's hard to find. I
recommend you call the Carroll County Historical Society at
(765) 564–3152 and tell them you have an arch fetish.

FINE FOR PARKING
East Chicago

It was once known as Indiana's "ideal city." And it may well be
the state's most unique city, the result of a visionary plan near
the turn of the century to build the community of the future.

Marktown, a neighborhood of East Chicago, is surrounded
by factories and an oil refinery. It doesn't look like a city that
started out as a quaint little burg, modeled after a Tudor-style
English village. It all began in 1917 when industrialist Clayton
Allen decided that his workers would be healthier and happier
if he could provide them with safe, affordable housing. Allen
hired Chicago architect Howard Van Doren Shaw, whose vision
of utopia was based on English garden city designs. Van Doren

Park on the sidewalk, walk in the street. Only in Marktown (and Manhattan).
PHOTO: Howard Van Doren Shaw Society, Paul A. Meyers, Executive Director

Shaw built Tudor-style homes with distinctive double-gable stucco walls with soft pastel colors. He envisioned narrow lanes (VERY narrow) with open streetside porches, so people could walk along the road and talk to neighbors. No alleys, no private garages. All very strange by today's standards.

This grand idea was interrupted by World War I, when only about 15 percent was completed. Those initial 100 buildings and 200 homes still stand today. And people still live in this historic community of 600, including Paul Myers, whose family has lived there for five generations. "It's the Brigadoon of industrial housing . . . a diamond in the rough awaiting restoration for future generations," he says.

How strange is this little hamlet? *Ripley's* made it an entry several years ago as "the only place in America where people park on the sidewalk and walk in the street."

To get to Marktown, take U.S. 80/94 to Cline Avenue, just north of the Riley exit. Go right on Riley Road about a quarter mile to Marktown. Walk the streets and you'll find someone that would love to tell you all the details. Or visit www. marktown.org

BURIED TREASURE
Frankfort

How would you like to see a wheelchair used by Franklin Roosevelt? What about Jack Benny's Maxwell? Or maybe the Leslie Special from the movie, *The Great Race*? Well, here's the neat part. You don't have to go to the Smithsonian Institution in Washington, D.C. You can just go to Frankfort, Indiana. To a funeral home.

Bill Miller's incredible collection of antique cars, bikes, toys, gas pumps, baby buggies, and hearses was started by his grandfather, William Goodwin, in the early 1950s. And that William Goodwin was the grandson of George William Goodwin, who opened a mortuary in Frankfort in 1856.

Grandfather Goodwin's first acquisitions were horse-drawn funeral vehicles that were probably manufactured just before the turn of the century. The collection blossomed to include Deusenbergs, an Auburn Boatail, and a Cord, all luxury automobiles that were manufactured—along with 500 other makes—right here in Indiana. You can even see a unique collection of car licenses from the days when people made their own plates.

Bill Miller and his museum: Lincoln kept here.
And other lots of other neat stuff.

Bill Miller's grandfather died at age ninety-two, active till the very end and always keeping a special eye out for Abe Lincoln memorabilia and Wooton furniture. All of the antiques—cars included—were displayed in the funeral home until 1997, when the mortuary expanded.

Miller has moved most of his artifacts to a 3,000-square-foot garage right next door. While the collection is not open to the public, Miller loves to talk to people who have a genuine interest in history and his antiques, so if you call for an appointment, you might get lucky. While there, make sure you take a peek inside the historic funeral home to see the notice from the Hamilton County sheriff indicating his plan to impound John Dillinger's car. Yeah, right.

Frankfort is easy to find. From Indy, take I–65 to State Road 39 North to Frankfort. The Goodwin Funeral Home is at 200 South Main, right in the center of town. Or phone (765) 654–5533.

Getaway Vacation
Hammond

For many years, the John Dillinger Museum was located in Nashville, Indiana. Mind you, Dillinger never lived in Nashville, but he did bank there on occasion. But when founder Joe Pinkston, a Dillinger historian (and somewhat of an eccentric), died in 1996, the Indiana Welcome Center near Hammond in Lake County purchased the concept and many of the artifacts. And they've added to the collection.

According to Luke Weinman, communications director for the center, Dillinger allegedly did "a decent number of bank robberies in the area," which I guess is a compliment, at least to Dillinger. The 2,000-square-foot museum is interactive. Guests can sit in a replica of the Biograph Theatre (outside of which Dillinger was killed), experience a simulated bank robbery, and see an Essex Teraplane 8, a replica of Dillinger's car. You also can compare crime labs of the past and present or see clips of the very movie that Dillinger was watching just before he was gunned down.

There's also a waxed corpse of Dillinger. If you turn a little knob, the corpse lights up. Isn't that a nice touch?

Although the museum features Dillinger, its theme is that crime doesn't pay. But you do. It's four bucks to get in. It's worth it. In fact, it's a steal. Call (219) 989–7979 for details and directions.

BEAT IT

For almost fifty years Paul Spotts Emrick of Fulton County was the band director for Purdue University. Unlike fellow Fulton resident Elmo Lincoln, the first Tarzan of the movies, Emrick was not a chest beater, but a drum beater. In fact, he was directly responsible for creating the world's biggest drum, and a whole lot more.

Emrick first got on the bandwagon in 1904, when he entered Purdue as a freshman. His family's musical background served him well and while still a student in 1905, he was named the band's first official director. In 1907, after watching geese fly over his head, Emrick conceived the idea of marching bands forming letters with their units, an idea that became a mainstay of not just Purdue, but most marching bands in the country today.

Emrick knew that people loved drums and was savvy enough to realize that a huge drum would bring notoriety to the university. So in 1921 he worked with the Leedy Manufacturing Company of Indianapolis to create a drum that stands more than 10 feet tall on its carriage. At $800, the drum was considered a steal at the time and is still considered a bargain that's hard to beat. Actually, it's a bargain that's easy to beat.

You get the point. It is still recognized by many as the largest in the world and serves as a centerpiece for the Purdue "All-American" Marching Band. The drum's head, more than 7 feet in diameter, is made from Argentinean steer hides. Since 1937 the shell, constructed of solid maple, has been painted gold and decorated with glittery "diamonds." The drum weighs 300 pounds, 500 pounds with its carriage.

Thanks to Emrick and his three successors, Purdue University bands can boast several firsts:

- First to carry all colors of the Big 10 schools
- First to play the opposing team's fight song
- First to play at the Indy 500

- *First to play from a completely darkened football field, while being lit with tiny battery-operated lights*
- *First to play at Radio City Music Hall*
- *First to break military ranks to make a formation of any kind—the Block "P"*

And finally, Purdue University is the first school to have one of its band members go into outer space. In 1969, Neil Armstrong, who played baritone in Emrick's band, set foot on the moon. One giant step for man, one giant step for a band.

Author's note: There are some (mainly IU grads) who say the Walt Disney drum or the University of Texas drum is bigger. Let's just say there are lots of ways to measure a drum, and I'm not going to beat this to death.

HESSSSSSSSSSTON
Hesston

We know this a book for families, but we'd like to tell about one place that is very steamy. It's the 155-acre Hesston Steam Museum in Hesston. The board of directors is a little edgy about the word museum. "It has a bit of a stodgy connotation," says board member John Carpenter, "and this place is about as far from a typical museum as you can get." Boy, is it!

Indiana's best outdoor museum, as long as it doesn't lose steam.
PHOTO: Hesston Steam Museum

Visitors can ride any one of the three steam locomotives as well as see steam at work in dozens of other pieces of equipment, including a cider press, sawmill, traction engines, a ninety-two-ton crane, a huge marine engine, and the first power plant generator that provided energy for the city of La Porte. The pride of the museum is "The India," a Scottish-built locomotive featured in *Around the World in 80 Days.* The museum also features railroads of several different scales, including a train for kids to ride.

The Hesston Steam Museum is open weekends Memorial through Labor Day, then Sundays through October, when you can see the fall foliage. Then stop at the gift shop or hang around the train depot with other train enthusiasts and tourists and discuss the merits of really hot water. The museum also runs a Halloween and Christmas train, as well as a Labor Day weekend Steam and Power Show, which has been named one of Indiana's top-ten festivals.

From I–94, take the New Buffalo exit south toward La Porte on Highway 39 and follow the signs. Bring a picnic lunch, walk through the park, and blow off some steam. For details call (219) 872–5055 or see the Web site: www.hesston.org.

FREE DELIVERY
Highland

If you choose to spend your Sunday morning at the Hegewisch Church in Highland, you won't notice anything too unusual. Pastor Michael Thierer's sermon and the format of the service are, in his words, "quiet and conservative." But this church specializes in people who have been misled. Thierer's small congregation has been attracted to this ministry because of its worldwide reputation for delivering, well, deliverance—the result of a successful exorcism. First introduced to Hegewisch by internationally known Pastor Win Worley in the early 1970s, this ministry has served hundreds of believers over the past thirty years, many from thousands of miles away.

Pastor Worley, author of *Battling the Hosts of Hell—Diary of an Exorcist,* died in 1993, but Pastor Thierer has continued the tradition, stressing his desire to help those who have failed to find an answer to problems through the more traditional approaches. Thierer, who once struggled with a $2,000-a-week cocaine habit, believes that the devil is the root cause of most serious personal problems, medical and psychological. He laments the rather unrealistic and graphic depiction of exorcism as seen in the movies, but he admits to witnessing strong physical manifestations as a result of the procedure, including levitations. "Some people have to be held down," says Thierer. He also has little use for psychotherapy. "You can't counsel a demon out. They don't listen to you. They are very stubborn."

The church does not charge for exorcisms. (We wanted to mention that so you'd realize just how funny the title of this story is.) The church is at 8711 Cottage Grove Avenue. Call for deliverance: (219) 838–9410. Or see their Web site, www.hbcdelivers.org.

THE WHOLE TRUTH
Kentland

To the untrained eye, it's just a big, big hole in the ground. Of course, it *is* just a big hole in the ground. But it is also considered by many to be one of Indiana's unique geological features. The Kentland Dome is part of a functioning limestone

The hole truth in Kentland. Or what we have dug up so far.

PHOTO: Rogers Group, Inc.

quarry, the result of a one-mile-in-diameter meteorite that crashed to the earth about a hundred million years ago. Or so the experts say.

The curiosity is that unlike most craters, this hole has no crest, no outline of a crater. And in a typical meteorite impact, the hardest rock would be at the bottom of the crater. But the folks at Newton County Quarry claim that the hardest rock is at the top, suggesting huge forces from above or below the surface did some serious pushing around. And if you are interested in this stuff (like, you have rocks in your head), you should also know that the layers of rock in cases like this should be in a horizontal position, but in Newton they go every which way. I mean, go figure.

Most geology experts think the original meteorite must have pulverized, explaining why they have never found any remains of the huge mass. If you want to try and figure it out for yourself, the Kentland Dome (3 miles east of Kentland) is not officially open to the public, but with a phone call (219–474–5125) and some light pleading you can go out on the observatory platform. Gaping is permitted. After all, it's a gaping hole.

R E L I G I O N   T O   S P A R E
Knox

If religion is right up your alley, or you're just praying for a 300 game in bowling, have we got the place for you. Linda and Bill Stage of Knox have a rosary in their front yard. And the "beads" are made of bowling balls. The oversized rosary encircles a gazebo in the couple's side yard, enclosing a shrine of the Blessed Virgin Mary. In case you miss it, the letters BVM are emblazoned on the top of the structure and can be seen from the main road.

The fifty-nine bowling balls, divided into five colors to represent the five races of the world, is appropriately named the World Rosary of Peace. All the balls are connected by a plastic landscaping chain through eyehooks that have been set into the balls, thus giving the appearance of a real—albeit HUGE—rosary.

The idea for a giant rosary came in the late 1970s from Father Emil Bloch, pastor of Saint Thomas Aquinas, in Knox. No one is sure where the late priest got the idea, but some speculate that he was inspired by a somewhat similar work of art in the British Museum in London. Either that or the parish

*Religion scores big in Knox. A rosary
made of bowling balls.*

bowling tournament. Bloch engineered the design and construction himself, beginning with some donated bowling balls, then asked the Stages, who were friends and parishioners, to display the rosary in their yard.

The original dedication of the rosary was in September of 1989. Father Bloch passed away two years later, and now the Stages continue the September rededication celebration in honor of their friend. To see it for yourself, go to the 4200 block of West County Road 200 North in Knox. You can see it from the street. Although it will look like a lane.

SHORT STORY

It is a small wonder that Che Mah lived in Knox, a small town in Starke County. Che Mah was a small wonder himself, once reported to be the shortest man who ever lived. He towered under Tom Thumb, who reached 32 inches. Born in China in 1838, Che Mah was only 28 inches tall and tipped the scales (he was a very small tipper) at 40 pounds. He died in 1928 at the age of ninety.

P. T. Barnum saw him in London in 1880 and realized the marketing potential of the act. Later Che Mah traveled with Annie Oakley, Chief Sitting Bull, and other notables in Buffalo Bill Cody's Wild West Show.

Che Mah married a normal-sized woman and settled in Knox, where he owned property, was highly respected, and was considered a gentleman who never angered anyone. This was a good idea on his part. He did, however, anger his wife, who sued for divorce, complaining that Che Mah was jealous and abusive—just two of his shortcomings. Che Mah claimed his wife had ceased to perform her wifely duties. That's more than we need to know.

Pictures of Che Mah can be seen in the Starke County Historical Museum. For more information, call the Starke County Historical Society at (574) 772–4311.

A Doll of a Llama
Kokomo

Bea and Irv Kesling of Kokomo don't claim their square-dancing llamas and alpacas are candidates for the Arthur Murray Dance Studios, but for twenty years their four-legged hoofers have been kicking up a storm. Despite their journey from the towering Andes in Chile, the llamas and alpacas adapted well to their new environment. Okay, adapting is one thing, but allemanding is quite another.

Bea Kesling was struck one day by the regal and majestic posture often taken by the camelids (a name that includes both alpacas and llamas). She and Irv had been occasional square dancers and Bea wondered if a quick do-si-do with an alpaca might be fun.

Her idea was received with a fair bit of skepticism. And laughter. But her herds were well mannered and trainable. Bea was convinced that her idea would fly. And dance.

It wasn't long before they performed at a llama convention in Kentucky. Once word got out that the camelids were hot to trot, more than 4,000 people showed up for their first big dance back at the farm in Tipton. "I did seventy-one radio interviews that week," says Bea. "Everyone in the country knew about it."

The llamas and alpacas, tethered to the human dancer with a lead and halter, seem incredibly willing to cooperate with their Homo sapien partners. The animals allemande, do-si-do, and move to the center and bow, all to the delight of onlookers who are just dying to cut in. But they can't. The Keslings pick the human partners carefully beforehand, matching up temperament and personality wherever possible.

If you're flying overhead, you can recognize the Kesling farm from the air because the llamarina (that's a llama barn, of course) features colored shingles in the shape of llamas and alpacas. It's also easy to find on the ground, on U.S. 31, 2 miles south of Kokomo. Look for the white gazebo, which is a building, not a type of llama. Call for information at (765) 453–7070, or see the Web site: www.llamasandalpacas.com.

Big Ben
Kokomo

One is tempted to say this next story is no bull. But we're better than that. Anyway, it isn't bull, it's steer. Not just any steer, but the biggest steer in the known world—whatever that means. He's dead, by the way. Stuffed. So he now sits (er, stands) in Highland Park in Kokomo, where people actually come to see him.

When Old Ben was born in Miami County, he weighed 135 pounds (equal to several sacks of White Castles) before he even got started. At age four, he was two tons. By the time he slipped on the ice in 1910 and broke both his legs, Ben weighed close to 5,000 pounds (4,720 pounds to be exact, in case you're looking to break the ninety-three-year-old record).

Old Ben was shipped to Indy for his conversion to frankfurters and then given to a taxidermist for posterity. And he had a huge posterity. There's probably more to this story, but that's enough—you know what—for one day.

To see Ben, take the Atlantic Ocean to England, head for London . . . wait, that's Big Ben. You want Old Ben. Just take U.S. 31 north to Kokomo and ask for directions to Highland Park. Everyone knows where Old Ben is.

Where's the beef? In Kokomo. Lots of it.
PHOTO: Steph Mineart

FREE GAS . . . STATION
Lafayette

The Standard Oil gas station on the corner of Sixth and South Streets in Lafayette no longer sells gas. But it does dispense a healthy dose of nostalgia at a very reasonable price: free.

The station is now a museum, restored to look as it did in the 1930s when Standard Oil was one of thirty-three stations in town. Clyde "Jonesy" Jones leased the building from Standard and for forty years did a one-man show, filling tanks and fixing cars in his two-bay garage. The building was constructed with glazed brick on both the inside and outside (all four walls), which was unique in the world at the time. Only seven examples of this type of architecture remain today.

Over the years the building fell into disrepair until local businessman Don Stein mobilized volunteers from his company and engineered a sixty-one-day restoration project. Stein did extensive research into how the building used to look and solicited the help of eighty-year-old Clyde Jones, who remembered each person who had bought a piece of the Standard Oil station when its contents were auctioned off ten years earlier.

Old time gas station in Lafayette. Fill up on nostalgia.
PHOTO: Don Stein, Red Crown Museum

Virtually all the original artifacts, including the gravity-fed gasoline pumps, were located. Shingles for the top of the decaying roof were found in a Standard Oil warehouse. Almost all the signage is original. Inside the museum you'll find much of the memorabilia associated with the era, including cash registers, candy, film, and clocks. And classic cars.

With restoration completed in 1991, the tiny service station began attracting crowds and now plays host to 15,000 folks a year. The museum is open 24/7, but entry requires a phone call to one of the many volunteer hosts. Without a call, you can enjoy the outside of the museum in all its glory or peep through the windows and still get a good look at the past. With a call (765–742–0280), you can get inside. It's a gas.

Bowl Bound
Lafayette

Boilermaker Football Coach Joe Tiller envies Purdue's entomology department. Why? Because the entomologists participate in a bowl every year. This just bugs the heck out of Coach Tiller.

Entomologists have been playing in Purdue's Bug Bowl for the last eleven years. It doesn't garner prime-time coverage or draw a stadium-size crowd. But it was featured on CNN and does attract nearly 10,000 people. Two of the bowl's biggest draws are the cricket-spitting contest and the cockroach racing at "Roach Hill Downs." *Guinness* has even sanctioned cricket spitting as an official sport. The record, 32 feet ½ inch, is held by Dan Capps of Madison, Wisconsin, whose collection of tens of thousands of insects and his bug and butterfly tattoos certainly demonstrate his dedication to the sport.

After a stop at the insect petting zoo and an awkward attempt at the caterpillar canter (a three-person, six-legged race), hungry guests can visit a variety of beetle bistros to ingest a buffet of insects. Entomologist and cricket-connoisseur Tom Turpin likens chocolate-covered crickets to a popular snack. "Insects have a nutty taste to them," he says. "So it's just like eating chocolate-covered peanuts." Another booth invites all comers to a blind taste test. The challenge is to figure out which spice cake is made with . . . gulp . . . mealworms. (Just like Grandma used to make.) One past participant said that the Bug Bowl is a great way for entomologists to interact with people. With recipes like that, it's no wonder they need help honing their social skills.

For more information call the Entomology Department on the West Lafayette campus at (765) 494–4554. If no one answers, just keep calling. If you can't bug them, who can you bug?

NUDETON COUNTY
Lake Village

Mark Twain once said, "Clothes make the man. Naked people have little or no influence in society." The nudists at Sun Aura Resort may not be influential, but they don't mind. They're busy having too much fun.

Sun Aura, formerly known as Naked City, is a nudist retreat near Lake Village where "clothing is optional and nudity is encouraged." While strolling the grounds you may see naked hikers, nude couples shooting pool, topless women sharing recipes for Saturday's potluck dinner (a weekly resort happening), skinny-dippers at the resort's heart-shaped lake, and what may be the world's sexiest timepiece, a shapely woman's leg sundial, playfully bent with its toes pointing to the correct time. According to one employee, the sundial really works. For

In the gam of life, Lake Village sticks out above all others.
PHOTO: Steph Mineart

some odd reason, though, it takes men nearly three times longer than women to correctly tell what time it is. ("Clock? What clock?")

This adult playground is open year-round. Nude ice fishing has yet to be embraced by the members, but the Valentine's party and the country hoedown inside the heated clubhouse have become popular winter events. According to one Sun Aura employee, "There are plenty of cowboy hats, lots of boots, and lots of naked bodies." Garth Brooks never had it this good.

In the summer, members work on erasing tan lines or attend the crowning of Miss Sun Aura. Sorry guys. Since the pageant is open to the public, all of the beauty queens must wear clothes. Another popular event is the Sun Aura 500, where competitors exchange racing suits for birthday suits and speed around in golf carts. Racing buffs in the buff. Ya gotta love this.

Lake Village is 10 miles west of Roselawn and I–65. For more information, call (219) 345–2000. They don't answer the phone all the time, so keep your shirt on.

PILLAR TALK
Lebanon

The people of Lebanon don't take their courthouse completely for granted. Nor do they take it for completely granite. The courthouse is also part Indiana limestone and contains eight huge limestone pillars, said to be the largest one-piece limestone columns in the world—almost 36 feet high and weighing 60,000 pounds each. The limestone was shipped to Lebanon from Bedford by train at the turn of the century, then transported on log rollers from the depot by some very unhappy horses. The columns were carved on the grounds, then lifted by a combination of steam and donkey power. Completed in 1912, the total cost of the courthouse—which also sports a beautiful marble rotunda and exquisite limestone carvings above the portals—was $325,000, a fraction of what a recent renovation cost.

Look up as you gaze upon the columns and you may see yet another surprise. Living on the roof of the courthouse is Socks, the cat. No relation to the former president's cat, but politically well placed nonetheless. Socks has lived on the roof for several years, the second feline to accept the job of ridding it of pigeons. Don't worry, Socks is well cared for, has her own little cat house, and is fed a standard diet, occasionally supplemented by a slow squab. She's also not confined to the roof but can come and go as she pleases, especially in bad weather. When not on patrol, Socks suns herself on the courthouse rotunda. And in case you're wondering, Socks is an independent, like all cats.

To find the courthouse, take I–65 north and get off at the second Lebanon exit. Go about 50 heading toward town and a nice police officer will take you right to the courthouse. I know. That's how I found it.

Killer Pillar in Lebanon, Indiana.

HOOSIER APE MAN

I Tarzan.

No. I Tarzan.

No. I Tarzan, and this Jane.

Will the real Tarzan please stand up? If you were asking the Indiana contingent of Ape Men to stand, three Tarzans would rise—and even one Jane.

Elmo Lincoln (Elmo Linkenhelt) holds the honor of being the first Tarzan. The broad-chested bruiser from Rochester was cast as the first vine-swinging, clipped-speaking ape man in the 1918 silent movie, Tarzan of the Apes. He was discovered while filming a fight scene for an earlier movie. When his shirt was ripped off, the director noticed his rippling chest and later gave Lincoln the role of the scantily clad jungle defender.

Dennis "Denny" Miller (aka Scott Miller) earned the honor of being the first blonde Tarzan. Born in Bloomington, the basketball standout originally went to Hollywood to play for the legendary UCLA coach and fellow Hoosier John Wooden. Upon graduating, he turned down an offer to turn pro, and he went into acting. He starred in Tarzan the Ape Man (1959).

Apparently, James "Babe" Pierce took the role of Tarzan to heart. The Freedom native not only costarred with Jane, but he was married to her. His first role as the ape man was in the 1927 movie, Tarzan and the Golden Lion. Later he married Joan Burroughs (the daughter of Tarzan's creator, Edgar Rice Burroughs), and from 1932 to 1934, he and his wife played Tarzan and Jane on the radio serial that aired in the United States, South America, and Europe.

Pierce and his wife are buried in Shelbyville. Their gravestones are engraved "Tarzan" and "Jane."

Who says Hoosiers aren't swingers?

CIRCLE CITY
Logansport

We could go round and round discussing where the most exquisite carousel in America is, but our vote goes to the Cass County Carousel in Riverside Park in Logansport.

Is it the most beautiful carousel in the world?
See for yourself. Just get in line.
PHOTO: T. J. Smith Studio

The hand-carved, 42-animal menagerie arrived in Logansport in 1919 from its original home in Fort Wayne. Its carver, Gustav Dentzel, was a German immigrant who settled in Philadelphia and made a name for himself as one of the world's finest carousel craftsmen. While records of the carousel can be traced back to 1902, there is evidence that some of the carved animals date back even further. One hint is that the horses, reindeer, lion, tiger, and goats have a pleasant visage, and Dentzel's style apparently changed after the turn of the century when he began creating a more menacing look. "We have the happy ones," says Betty Steinhilber, the operations director for the carousel.

The carousel, now designated as a National Historic Landmark, is housed in its own climate-controlled building, removed from the elements that once almost ruined it. A major restoration several years ago brought the animals back to life and even uncovered—literally—the fact that a black panther was really a tiger.

What a ride for 50 cents! And as you revolve around the ship's mast in the center of the carousel, everyone has a chance to grab at silver rings. But only one lucky rider snatches the brass ring. And that gives you a free ride. To try for the ring yourself, travel north on U.S. 31 from Indianapolis to U.S. 24 West to Logansport. The carousel is in Riverside Park, and it's open daily Memorial Day through Labor Day and on weekends through October. But times vary, so you might want to call ahead: (574) 753–8725.

RISING POSTAL RATES

*U*sually the "first" of anything is a hotly contested claim. But most mail historians (and fe-mail, too) agree that the very first official air mail flight in a balloon took place in August of 1859 between Lafayette and Crawfordsville. Problem is, that was not the intended route.

The "mailman" was airman John Wise, a noted balloonist of his day who had actually tried unsuccessfully earlier in his career to deliver a letter from St. Louis to New York. A crash landing burst his bubble, but Wise didn't give up. Months later he attempted still another flight, this time with 123 stamped letters on board his balloon Jupiter, along with a small cadre of scientific apparatuses. Destination: New York City. Wise headed out from Lafayette where westerly winds would be at his back—he thought. Instead, he encountered a southerly wind and 91 degree temperature, enough to force a landing only 30 miles from Lafayette.

So why is this considered the first airmail delivery? Because Wise stopped a passing train and transferred his postal pack to the railroad, which successfully delivered the mail days later. And so, one leg of the journey was indeed by air. Regular airmail delivery did not occur again for seventy years. Some think a balloon would still be faster. But this first official airmail flight was recognized as such by the United States Post Office with a commemorative stamp on its hundredth anniversary.

CRANING YOUR NECK
Medaryville

Those who would contend that Jasper County is for the birds have obviously enjoyed one of the most majestic sights in the Hoosier State. On a clear day in late October or November, you may not be able to see Chicago, but you can see as many as 16,000 migrating sandhill cranes as they take a respite in Jasper-Pulaski Fish and Wildlife Area, feed in the shallow marsh, and then go on to raid the cornfields.

An adult sandhill crane is 4 to 5 feet tall with a wing span to 7 feet. The sandhill has grayish plumage and red patches on the head. Often mistaken for a heron, these elegant birds represent one of the oldest bird species, dating back over two million years. How to tell the difference? Cranes fly with their necks stretched out, herons tuck the head back. Cranes have loud trumpet calls, while herons have low hoarse croaks.

This stop along the cranes' migration trail from points north is eons old and was in danger in the 1930s, when their numbers severely decreased, probably due to human encroachment, as well as being shot and sold for food. With government protection in recent years, the number of cranes has risen dramatically. The birds, who know a good bed-and-breakfast when they see one, pass the tradition along to their offspring.

The cranes stick around for a couple of months, then head south for Georgia and Florida. Cranes also stop in Jasper-Pulaski in the spring, but October, November, and December are the prime viewing months and spectators flock from all over to see the birds that have, well, flocked here themselves. Best time to look and listen is at dawn when they spring from the roosting marshes and call out in unison; then again at sunset when they return for the evening. Those who know, like

Jim Bergens of the Department of Natural Resources, suggest watching the cranes from the Goose Pasture viewing area.

Jasper-Pulaski Fish and Wildlife Area is 5 miles north of Medaryville on U.S. 421, about 40 miles south of Michigan City. We may be sticking our neck out here, but this is one of Indiana's great natural treasures. For more info call (219) 843–4841.

HEAVEN CAN WAIT
Monticello

Some people are driven by their religious fervor. Others drive themselves. That's true of the congregation at the Monticello United Methodist Church where, every Sunday morning during the summer months, the Reverend Wes Brookshire and his associates hold a service at the local drive-in theater. Worshipers here are equally concerned with a place in heaven as a space in the parking lot.

The tradition started in Monticello more than twenty years ago, when the Reverend Ed Helm of the United Methodist Church borrowed the idea from TV evangelist Robert Schuller, who began his own career at a drive-in and then pioneered the concept of outdoor services.

Here's how it works: A pickup truck pulls a wagon equipped with a pulpit and sound equipment. The wagon has a shelter built on it that is affectionately called the "coop," as in chicken coop. The congregation can hear the sermon and music on their car radio via a special frequency in the parking area. Brookshire is not projected on the screen, but most people can see him. "But I can't see them," admits Brookshire. "The windshield is a problem, but you get used to it."

Driving home the word of God.

PHOTO: Monticello United Methodist Church

Because Monticello is home to nearby Indiana Beach, the idea of praying to the Son before heading for the sun seemed a natural. On a typical Sunday morning, more than fifty cars drive into the lot, many filled with entire families and their pets. People often pray while munching on breakfast sandwiches and sipping coffee. But the service is interactive. The congregation, for example, is encouraged to toot their horns when it's time to say Amen. I wish we were making this up.

The service is free to the public, but they do pass a Kentucky Fried Chicken Bucket for donations. Let's just call it a wing and a prayer. Interested in going to a service? From Lafayette take State Road 43 North to U.S. 24, then go east to Monticello. Or call (574) 583–5545 and see what's praying.

GOING POSTAL
Peru

Drive on up U.S. 31 one evening, just north of Grissom Air
Force Base, where you may be distracted by a cacophony of
lights punctuating the evening air. Fighter pilots going on a
mission? Nope. Training maneuvers for new cadets? Wrong
again. Maybe it's the circus. Everyone knows that Peru is
famous for its circus. But that's why it's not in this book.
Everyone knows about it.

No, this is the largest collection of ready-to-go lampposts
and lamppoles (we don't know the difference, either) in the

Too many lamp posts, not enough drunks in Peru.

Midwest, some say the United States. Paul Knebel of P. K. Distributors has been selling sand-cast aluminum products for more than twenty years. We don't know what that means, but it's apparently a good thing. His shop, just off U.S. 31, has more than 500 lampposts, more than an entire town of drunks could hope for.

The aluminum castings come from Mexico, but Knebel mixes and matches parts so that, unlike most super-hardware stores, he gives you a hundred different choices instead of four or five. Don't need a lamppost? How about an eagle, a Statue of Liberty, a library lion, or an elephant? Buy that fountain that you've dreamed of. What the heck, get that suit of armor you have always wanted. If you can't find what you want at P. K.'s, they probably don't make it.

Knebel says that his roadside location creates a lot of traffic—people intrigued by what they see as they barrel down the highway. The evening hours can get especially crowded. "I think that humans are attracted by the light," says Knebel. This is one of those places that's easy to find and hard to miss. It's just 3 miles north of Grissom Air Force base on the east side of U.S. 31. The Web site is www.pkdist.com. Or give a call at (765) 472–0369. They'll keep the light on for you.

FOUNTAIN OF KNOWLEDGE
Remington

You won't find Remington in most tourism books. No sun-kissed beaches, no floating casinos, not one Elvis impersonator. But every summer people flock here, to the Fountain Park

Chautauqua, the only remaining continuously running chautauqua in Indiana and one of the few left in the United States.

More than a hundred years old, the chautauqua movement is a kind of floating band of educators, entertainers, and ministers who brought the city to rural America. People would travel from nearby towns and pitch tents to hear such famous guest speakers as William Jennings Bryant, who mesmerized the crowds and then went on to the next location. Although the movement became much less popular as the automobile gained in popularity and the culture of a city was only a drive away, a handful of chautauquas still remain today.

The Fountain Park Chautauqua is planned locally and, unlike other chautauquas, there are permanent residences, dozens of cottages built decades ago so folks could enjoy guaranteed access to two weeks of entertainment, educational classes, and fellowship. Those cottages remained in families so each new generation could come and enjoy the festivities, no matter where they lived.

Those without cottages enjoy the Fountain Park Hotel, a grand building with thirty-six rooms and a 136-seat dining room. The hotel, built in 1898, is open only two weeks a year. To re-create the feeling of the past, the ruling committee voted that air-conditioning would not be installed. Oh, and there is no alcohol. And no phones or TV. And it's still impossible to get a room. We hope this concept doesn't catch on.

The Fountain Park Chautauqua has not missed a meeting in more than a century. Start your own streak by visiting the grounds the last week in July and the first week in August. The Remington Chautauqua is a mile north and a half mile west of Remington near the intersection of State Roads 231 and 24. By the way, a few Indiana cities—we won't mention any names—call their annual festivals chautauquas 'cause it sounds cool. That doesn't count. If there ain't no history, there ain't no mystery.

WORLD'S FASTEST

*F*ly over the tiny town of Oxford and you'll see the numbers 1:55 painted atop a tiny structure just on the edge of town. This is Benton County's testimony to Dan Patch, possibly Indiana's greatest athlete. The 1:55 represents Patch's lightning speed in a mile run, a record that stood for thirty-two years. But the story of Dan Patch is more than just numbers.

The story behind this great athlete began here, in little Oxford, where Patch was born with a crooked leg that required him to have assistance just to stand. By the time the little guy was four years old, he was already wowing people with his amazing speed and his desire to compete. He even won his first race. By 1903 many sports enthusiasts considered young Dan Patch the fastest in the world and he was soon the undisputed world champion.

In the course of Patch's career, he never lost a race and set dozens of records. Those who watched him run said, "He would pass others like they were standing still." He was also probably the first athlete to be marketed worldwide. Way before icons like Babe Ruth, Patch's image was used to sell cigars, watches, sleds, toys, gasoline engines, even cars. Patch's lifetime earnings were in the neighborhood of two million dollars, an unheard of number in the early 1900s.

Like Michael Jordan today, Patch was a giant among athletes. He had his own railway car and when he went to a new city, throngs of admirers came out to see him. Sportswriters wrote about his intelligence and love of music. But he had his dark side. He never talked to reporters, never signed an autograph. Except for a chosen few, Patch never really warmed up to most people.

*Dan Patch died in 1916 as a result of heart problems.
People mourned the loss of this great athlete. There was even
some speculation he would be stuffed and mounted.*

*Dan Patch, you see, was a harness racehorse. And now
you know the rest of the story.*

Where is it in Benton County? Just ask. Everyone knows.

Dan Patch slept here. Standing up.

PHOTO: Oxford Memorabilia

BACK TO THE FIFTIES
Sharpsville

Jim Richardson of Sharpsville spent more than a few years of his life driving around the Indiana countryside trying to relive his days as a kid. "Over every crest in the hill, I hoped to look down on a little town just like the one I grew up in back in the fifties."

No such luck, so the Sharpsville resident decided to build his own. Neighbors and friends questioned his sanity, but Richardson lost no time drawing up a series of detailed blueprints for a town complete with gasoline station, firehouse, diner, and barbershop. He called it Summerplace.

With the help of friends and other volunteers, he began collecting artifacts from the 1950s. Inside his gas station, for example, along with vintage cars and bikes, are cans of 1950s motor oil, spark plug boxes, tools, TV sets, and magazines. Outside the building are stoplights, gas pumps, product signs, streetlamps, and a movie marquee, all from the 1950s of his childhood. Some of the memorabilia has been refurbished, but it is all original. No exceptions.

Summerplace is open by appointment to special groups, and Richardson has a special place in his heart for older folks who want to reconnect with a lost time. "I've had senior citizens sit in this garage and weep. It allowed them to get back in touch with their youth."

Richardson has paid a price for his hard work: several broken bones, cracked ribs, and heat exhaustion. But still, he calls the days of his youth and his re-creation the "fabulous fifties." Sharpsville is just south of State Road 26 and east of U.S. 31. But you can't really see Summerplace from the street, so you'd better call (765) 963–5943.

The good ol' days. Still available in Sharpsville.

RAY EWRY

Raymond Ewry is not exactly a household name. Not like Reggie Miller or Bobby Knight. But he should be.

Born in Lafayette Raymond C. Ewry was stricken by polio while just a small boy. In the 1880s he was confined to a wheelchair. Many thought he would never walk again. But Ewry was placed on a rigid exercise program and he fought back tirelessly, first walking, then running, and finally jumping.

In 1890 he entered Purdue University, where he excelled in football and ran track. That wasn't enough. In 1900, at age 27, he went to Paris for the Olympics. There he took gold medals in the high jump, standing triple jump, and standing long jump. His nickname: The Human Frog. Ewry went on to three more Olympic Games, in St. Louis, Athens, and London. All together, he won ten gold medals, still a record today.

Very few people have ever heard the name Ray Ewry. We hope we have changed that.

BIRD'S EYE VIEW
South Bend

The trees in Bendix Woods just outside of South Bend don't spell trouble. But they do spell S-T-U-D-E-B-A-K-E-R. And they have for almost seventy years. Although you wouldn't know that unless you flew over them.

The idea sprouted in the 1930s, when the Studebaker Corporation was looking for a promotional gimmick that would both advertise their company and capitalize on the nation's love affair with flight. And so, after a Studebaker engineer got out his slide rule and plotted the coordinates, the company planted 8,000 red and white pine seedlings. Seventy-five years later, the trees are 70 to 80 feet tall and were listed in the *1987 Guinness Book of Records* as the longest living sign in the world. That's a half mile long and 200 feet wide—as the crow flies.

When Studebaker went out of business, the land was purchased by the Bendix Corporation, which deeded some of the property to the St. Joseph County Parks Department. In 1978, when the Parks Department also acquired St. Patrick's County Park, volunteers just went out of their tree trying to resurrect the Studebaker concept. And so, now you can see both S-T-U-D-E-B-A-K-E-R and S-T. P-A-T-R-I-C-K from your Cessna. C-O-O-L, H-U-H?

DUNN DEAL
Tefft

A philosopher once said, "Legend is the bridge to truth." But sometimes, it's the bridge that's the legend. Dunn's Bridge, just north of the tiny town of Tefft, has been the center of more than a little controversy for over a hundred years.

The story begins in 1893 in Chicago, site of the World's Fair, also known as the Columbian Exposition. People in the Windy City, indeed the entire nation, were abuzz about a new amusement ride that would debut at the international event. George Ferris, folks say, had once scribbled his notion for this outrageous piece of machinery on a dinner napkin in Chicago after being challenged by a friend to design something that rivaled the Eiffel Tower. Many believe Ferris succeeded. His engineering feat thrilled the nation and lifted the spirits of the 2,000-plus people who sat in the wheel each trip.

That's not a misprint: 2,000 people per trip!

Ferris, with the help of Luther Rice, a Hoosier construction engineer, enjoyed great success with his ride for several years, but in 1906 the cost of maintaining the machine was so enormous that the wheel was dynamited and sold for scrap.

Where did the scrap metal go? Some say it went to Hoosier Isaac Dunn, who used some of the metal frame to construct a bridge across the Kankakee River. Well, that's what some folks say. The controversy continues. Some say the bridge is made from the original Ferris Wheel, some say it isn't. Some say the story's all true; some say it's all malarkey. Some say it's half true.

Well, we could go round and round in circles on this and accomplish nothing. That's the way George Ferris would have liked it. To ride the bridge yourself, call (219) 866–5433 and ask for directions.

ROCKY START
Thorntown

In 1982 Bud Moody had a vision: Build it and they will pray. So the good reverend began a yearlong project constructing a prayer garden and chapel with stones he found at an abandoned rest stop.

As the tiny band of parishioners assisted Moody in his mission, nearby farmers and passing truckers stopped not only to gape but to gather rocks and donate money. No one really had any experience building anything like this, but that didn't stop the congregation from digging in.

Rock of Ages: the favorite hymn in Thorntown.

When the prayer garden and chapel were complete, a church was also built to serve the tiny community. They had been conducting services in a small building in Thorntown, but now the Full Gospel Church had a new home.

The Walnut Grove Church has about thirty-five in the congregation, but Reverend Ryan Glauber feels he reaches the masses. "We have people from all over the country stop by and sign our prayer book in the chapel," says Glauber.

The stone chapel is adjacent to the Thorntown exit on U.S. 52 and is visible from the road. Stop by, sign the book, and leave a few coins.

HOOSIER HOOPS
Wingate

B asketball fans may be surprised. But true basketball historians know all about it. It's all on a sign on Indiana Highway
25 proclaiming the town of Wingate as the home of the Indiana
state basketball champions in 1913 and 1914. That's back-to-
back championships twenty-five years before Bobby Plump put
Milan High School on the map. And then in 1920, this same
team from the tiny town of Wingate won the national basketball championships in Chicago. Didn't know that, did you?

Both Crawfordsville and Wingate had been cited by the
IHSAA in 1920 for using players outside their school district.
Banned from official league play, the two high schools fought
independent teams and played unsanctioned games. But they
were so good that when the national championships were held
in Chicago, they were asked to play anyway. The final game:
Wingate 22, Crawfordsville 10.

That's a long time ago, when backboards and bottomless nets
were innovations and the game was only just beginning to stir
the passions of Hoosiers. But this is where basketball was
brought to the Crawfordsville area in 1893 by an assistant of
James Naismith, the man who invented the game in Massachusetts just two years earlier. Naismith himself would visit Indiana in 1925 and say, "Basketball really started here in Indiana,
which remains the center of the sport."

The Wingate players did not have a real gym, just a stable
that later was converted to a basketball court. You can look for
that original barn if you're in Wingate (just west of Crawfordsville), but it would only depress you. Today it's back to
being a barn, apparently safe from being destroyed, but waiting for a benefactor to restore it—and history at the same time.
The first electric scoreboard, built by two locals, debuted in this
gym. No one knows where it is today.

WHAT A CARD . . . COLLECTION
Zionsville

If you ever meet insurance agent John Haffner of Zionsville and you offer him your business card, he'll take it. Not that he needs it. John has eight million of them in his basement. In boxes. In plastic bags. In three-ring binders. Incredible.

The origin of this massive collection is quite a story. Here's what we know. Or think we know. Maybe. It begins about twenty years ago in England where a little boy named Craig Shergold was hospitalized with cancer. When the youngster began getting get-well cards, hospital employees and friends struck up the idea to try for a spot in the *Guinness Book of World Records*.

The story was picked up on a number of wire services. And there was a chain letter. By then Shergold himself learned what his friends had orchestrated and was a willing participant in the idea. Millions of get-well cards arrived, but that's just half the story.

Somewhere along the line, the request for get-well cards turned into business cards. No one is sure how or why, although some suggest it was a ruse to acquire a mailing list. It could have just been a miscommunication. In addition, the word spread that the whole thing was being run by the Children's Make-a-Wish Foundation out of Atlanta. It wasn't true.

Before long, truckloads of business cards were making their way to Atlanta. It was ugly for a while. The post office didn't want to store them. Make-a-Wish didn't want to accept them. The last thing Craig Shergold wanted was more cards. He had already broken the get-well card record.

Ultimately, 20 million of these cards were "accepted" by Walter Day of Iowa, an investigator for *Guinness* and collector himself. Even Day was overwhelmed by the amount. Which gets us to John Haffner, Boone County resident, who also had a passion for business cards and decided he'd like part of the collection. He flew to Iowa, rented a truck, and brought eight million cards back to his home in Zionsville toward the end of 2002.

Haffner admits that he, too, was overwhelmed by the enormity of what he had. Normally, he categorizes the cards (baseball players, CIA agents, Disney employees, people named Bob, etc.—the list is endless), but this was a task of inconceivable proportions.

So is Haffner going to go through eight million cards to see what he has? "Not if I want to keep my family," says Haffner, who is looking for other collectors to whom he can offer one of his thousand or so bags/boxes of unsorted—sometimes wet and crumpled—business cards.

Want a box of 10,000? They're free. Just pay for shipping and handling, which comes to about $25. And you thought there were no good deals anymore. Haffner's E-mail address is HAF705490@aol.com.

INDEX

ABOUT THE AUTHOR

Dick Wolfsie has been a household name for twenty years. Okay, maybe not in your household, but in his.

He has taught high school and college, hosted three TV talk shows and one radio show, and has written three books. In Indiana alone, he's interviewed more than 15,000 people and done more than 5,000 hours of live radio and television. That's why he is always so tired.

Dick has earned two national entertainment awards, a regional Emmy, and a dozen local awards, but he can't find any of them. Same with his keys and his wallet.

PHOTO: The Picture People

In order to write this book, he drove several thousand miles throughout Indiana. He also drove some in Kentucky, Ohio, and Illinois, but not on purpose.

Dick has been accompanied everywhere he goes—including work—by his faithful beagle, Barney. He has been a reporter on WISH–TV Channel 8 in Indianapolis for the last ten years, which is the longest tenure Dick has ever had at any station without getting fired. He should have thought of this dog thing a long time ago.

Dick's next book is *Modern Day Houdini* (The Globe Pequot Press, 2003). It's a collaboration with Bill Shirk, the World's Number One Escape Artist (see pp. 44–45), and in it all of his secrets are revealed—Bill's, not Dick's.

Dick lives in Indianapolis with his wife, Mary Ellen, and Brett, his son. He would be lost without them.